Fourth Class
Primary 6

VERITAS

Grow in Love Series
Published by
Veritas Publications
7–8 Lower Abbey Street
Dublin 1, Ireland

publications@veritas.ie
www.veritas.ie

ISBN 978 1 84730 791 0

Copyright © Council for Catechetics of the Irish
Episcopal Conference, 2017

10 9 8 7 6 5 4 3 2 1

The material in this publication is protected by
copyright law. Except as may be permitted by
law, no part of the material may be reproduced
(including by storage in a retrieval system) or
transmitted in any form or by any means, adapted,
rented or lent without the written permission of
the copyright owners. Applications for permissions
should be addressed to the publisher.

A catalogue record for this book is available from
the British Library.

Veritas books are printed on paper made from the
wood pulp of managed forests. For every tree felled,
at least one tree is planted, thereby renewing natural
resources.

Original illustrations: Norma Prause Brewer
Art direction & design: Lir Mac Cárthaigh
Design & layout: Heather Costello

See page 110 for copyright acknowledgements.

Printed in Ireland by Boylan Print Group,
Drogheda

Welcome to Grow in Love

Dear Families,
Welcome to *Grow in Love* for Fourth Class/Primary 6. This year we begin by once again emphasising for the children that God loves them always, unconditionally, and that God created the world and everything in it out of love. We revise the story of Creation, which the children have already heard throughout the *Grow in Love* series. We introduce them to the covenant that God made with his people through Noah, Abraham and Moses, each of whom responded with faith and trust. God calls us, too, to respond to his call with the same faith and trust.

In this year's theme on the Bible we focus on the New Testament. We provide a brief introduction to the books of the New Testament, particularly the four Gospels. We also emphasise the reverence with which Christians have treated the Bible through the ages. We explore the Book of Kells as an example of the extraordinary efforts made by ancient scribes to produce a manuscript worthy of the Word of God.

From the beginning God the Father promised to send his Son, Jesus, to teach us about himself and to show us how he wants us to love him and one another. The children will hear a number of Bible stories from the life of Jesus, with a particular emphasis on the parables of Jesus. They will also explore what it means to be a missionary.

We look at how people of faith down through the ages have responded to God's call, from Abraham in the Old Testament to all those who serve in local parish communities today. We introduce the Fourth, Fifth, Seventh, Eighth and Tenth Commandments and we help the children to begin to see how they, too, can respond to God's call by living according to these Commandments and by observing Jesus' Commandment of Love. We guide the children to be more aware of the need to care for the earth and we alert them to Jesus' call to be respectful of all people and their rights. We assure the children that God will help them to live as Jesus has asked them to, and that, if they fail, God is always ready to forgive them. We look at the Sacrament of Reconciliation at a deeper level than in previous programmes. The children will explore the dynamics of forgiveness and their own need to forgive others.

The children will hear more stories about St Brigid and explore the richness of the faith of those who lived in early Christian Ireland. They will also learn more about the tradition of pilgrimage in the Church today and about places of pilgrimage in Ireland and abroad.

We continue to provide opportunities for the children to participate in vocal and meditative prayer and we help them to be aware that, when they pray, God is always listening to them. We introduce *lectio divina* (divine reading) as a way of praying using Scripture.

As well as exploring further the beliefs and practices of the Catholic Church, we introduce the children to some of the beliefs and practices of the Methodist, Presbyterian, Church of Ireland and Orthodox Churches. Each year we introduce the children to other non-Christian faiths in a manner appropriate to their age. This year we focus on Islam.

Throughout this book you will find activities that you can do each week to support the work that the teacher is doing in school. We encourage you to take this opportunity to teach your child about the faith that you chose for him or her in Baptism. We hope that, with the support of the teachers in your school and of your parish community, this programme can help you as you journey with your child to 'grow in love' of God and of others.

Welcome to *Grow in Love*!

IN SCHOOL

THIS WEEK IN SCHOOL

You are invited to think about:
- How God's plan for your life is unfolding
- Giving thanks to God for the gift of life and all creation
- How you can use your gifts and talents to care for and protect God's creation

KEY WORDS

Genesis: The name given to the first book in the Bible.

Covenant: Agreement.

Angels: Messengers of God who worship God and serve him.

THEME 1: GOD | LESSON 1

God Has a Plan for Us

ABOUT BEGINNINGS

New beginnings are important. It is both exciting and challenging to begin something new, whether that be a new year in school, or something new happening in our home, our club or our neighbourhood. We began our life in God's family when we celebrated the Sacrament of Baptism.

The Bible, our Sacred Scripture, begins with the story of how God created the world and everything in it. This helps people of faith to believe that God has a plan for every part of creation and especially for every person.
- How do you feel about God having a plan for your life?
- What does knowing that God has a plan for everyone teach you about God?

Read this passage from the Book of Genesis about God's work of Creation:

> **The Story of Creation (Genesis 1:3-5, 24-28, 31)**
>
> Then God commanded, 'Let there be light' – and light appeared. God was pleased with what he saw. Then he separated the light from the darkness, and he named the light 'Day' and the darkness 'Night'. Evening passed and morning came – that was the first day...
>
> Then God commanded, 'Let the earth produce all kinds of animal life: domestic and wild, large and small' – and it was done. So God made them all, and he was pleased with what he saw.
>
> Then God said, 'And now we will make human beings; they will be like us and resemble us. They will have power over the fish, the birds, and all animals, domestic and wild, large and small.' So God created human beings, making them to be like himself. He created them male and female, blessed them, and said, 'Have many children, so that your descendants will live all over the earth and bring it under their control. I am putting you in charge of the fish, the birds, and all the wild animals'... God looked at everything he had made, and he was very pleased. Evening passed and morning came – that was the sixth day.

REFLECT

Take time to reflect on the seven words you chose and the images you drew in your zigzag book about the story of Creation as it is told in the Book of Genesis.

Grow in Love | Fourth Class/Primary 6

IN SCHOOL

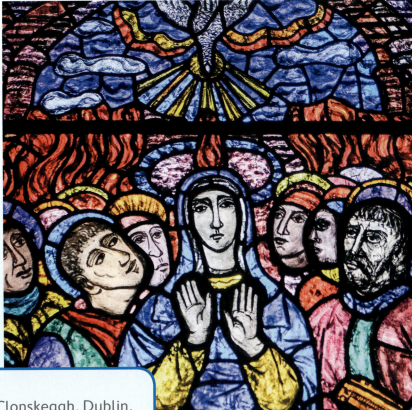

Pentecost by Evie Hone (1946)

Fact file: Evie Hone

Evie Hone (1894–1955) was born in Clonskeagh, Dublin. She came from a family of artists.

At the age of twelve Evie contracted polio. This left her with severe lameness for the rest of her life. Despite this, she was determined to study art and she began attending classes in London. Later, she did further study in Paris. The stained-glass windows of Chartres Cathedral and early Celtic art made a big impression on her imagination.

In 1925 Evie decided to enter religious life as a nun so as to dedicate her life to God. However, this did not work out and so she went to Holland and studied with a famous stained-glass artist, Professor Roland Holst.

When she returned to Ireland, Evie began to design her own stained glass. She was a woman of deep religious faith. Many of her beautiful stained-glass windows were inspired by passages from the Bible or scenes from the natural world. Her windows can be found in churches in different parts of Ireland. Perhaps you could arrange to visit one if it is close to where you live.

FOR MEMORISATION

Preface Dialogue
Priest: The Lord be with you.
People: And with your spirit.

Priest: Lift up your hearts.
People: We lift them up to the Lord.

Priest: Let us give thanks to the Lord our God.
People: It is right and just.

ACTIVITY

Imagine having a chance to talk to Evie Hone about her life and work. Act out the conversation with another pupil. Here are some questions to get you started:
- Evie, why do you like to work with stained glass?
- What inspires your work?
- What helps you to complete a piece of work?

Theme 1: God | Lesson 1: God Has a Plan for Us

AT HOME

DID YOU KNOW?
When we use our gifts and talents we can help to make God's plan a reality.

TIME TOGETHER

Chat Together
About the new beginnings that happened in your child's life – the day your child was born, spoke their first word, their first day at school, etc.

Read
Read together the passage from the Book of Genesis on page 4 of this book. It tells part of the story of Creation.

View
View some stained-glass windows together in a local church or online. What words would you use to describe them?

Invitation to Pray
God our Father, Creator of all life, help us to be aware of your divine plan unfolding in our lives each day. Guide us in our thoughts, words and actions to be your helpers, working to bring about your plan. We ask this through Jesus Christ our Lord. Amen.

Be Creative
Play your part in making God's plan a reality by helping to make good things happen in the world about you. Decide together on one thing you can do this week.

THIS WEEK
The children explored how new beginnings are important times. The biblical account of Creation offers us a sense of God's plan for the world and for human beings. God's plan for each of us continues to unfold with each new beginning in our lives.

Read the poem 'The New School Year' together.

The New School Year

The silent school all summer waits
So quiet and still behind the gates.
But now the gates are open wide
And all the teachers crowd inside.
(As they prepare to start their day,
The staffroom kettle steams away.)
The children come from far and near,
(Some junior infants shed a tear!)
It's time to start *the new school year.*

There will be laughter joy and fun
(And also homework to be done!)
And dressing up for Halloween
And sums like 10+17,
And Circle Time and Show and Tell
And running when you hear the bell,
And Christmas carols in the hall
(Perhaps a little snow may fall!)
And spelling tests and still more sums
(And asking '*An bhfuil cead agam?*')
Until at last the summer comes.
And then we'll go our separate ways
To start *the summer holidays.*

Grow in Love | Fourth Class/Primary 6

IN SCHOOL

THEME 1: GOD | LESSON 2

God's Promise to Abram

ABOUT PROMISES

Abram was a man of faith. He knew that God had kept his promises to Noah, his family and all creation. God made a promise to Abram in his old age. God promised that he would lead Abram to a new land and that he would give him the gift of descendants.

- Why do people make and keep promises? How would you describe a person who keeps their promises?
- Recall the story of the king and the promise he made to the poor criminal? How would you have advised the king to act in this story?
- Have you ever made a promise to someone and broken it? How did you feel? How do you think the other person felt?
- Recall the words you wrote on your rainbow mobile to remember the promises that God made to Noah and all creation.
- Why do you think Abram had such faith in God and his promises?
- How do you feel about the belief that God is faithful in keeping his promises to all his people?

ACTIVITY

- In your Religious Education journal write an acrostic poem using each letter of the word 'PROMISES' in sequence to begin each line.

THIS WEEK IN SCHOOL

You are invited to think about:
- The promise God made to Abram and his wife Sarai
- Giving thanks to God for being faithful to his promises
- Sharing how you grow into a deeper, trusting and faithful friendship with God

Theme 1: God | Lesson 2: God's Promise to Abram 7

IN SCHOOL

Read this passage from the Book of Genesis about God's promise to Abram and his wife Sarai:

God's Call to Abram (Genesis 12:1-2, 4-7)

The Lord said to Abram, 'Leave your country, your relatives, and your father's home, and go to a land that I am going to show you. I will give you many descendants, and they will become a great nation. I will bless you and make your name famous, so that you will be a blessing…'

When Abram was seventy-five years old, he started out from Haran, as the Lord had told him to do; and Lot went with him. Abram [also] took his wife Sarai…

When they arrived in Canaan… the Lord appeared and said to him, 'This is the country that I am going to give to your descendants.'

ABOUT CHANGE

In groups, talk about times when you experienced big changes in your life. Did you ever have to leave behind something that you treasured, like a favourite toy, teddy or item of clothing? How did you feel about that? Did you ever have to leave behind someone whom you really liked and felt comfortable with, like your childminder or your first teacher, because you were getting older and it was time for you to have new experiences, to learn new things and to meet new people? What was it like to leave those people and things behind and move on?

ACTIVITY

- Think about God's promise to be with you as you leave old and familiar situations and move to new and unknown experiences. Think about any concerns you may have in your life at this time.
- Share your thoughts with God. You might like to write a short prayer in your Religious Education journal about this experience.

IN GROUPS

- In small groups, take turns to recall stories of fictional characters who left their familiar lives to go on a journey in order to keep a promise they made to themselves or to someone else; for example, Harry Potter, the Wizard of Oz.

FOR MEMORISATION

The Lord is good;
  his love is eternal
  and his faithfulness lasts
    forever. (Psalm 100:5)

THIS WEEK
The children heard that God keeps his promises to us, even when we turn away from him. They explored how the stories in the beginning of the Book of Genesis, such as the story of Adam and Eve, reveal God's plan for creation. They know that Noah, and Abram and Sarai (whose names God changed to Abraham and Sarah) were invited to place their trust in God, and that they did as God asked.

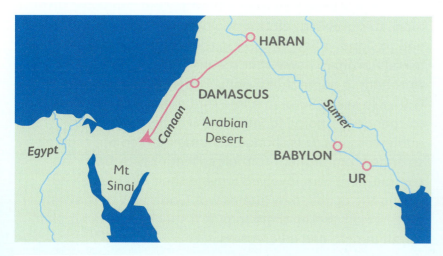

Abram had heard about God's covenant with Noah and he knew that God had kept his promise to Noah, his family and all of creation. Read about the promise that God made to Noah in this passage from the Book of Genesis:

God's Covenant with Noah (Genesis 9:8-11, 13)
God said to Noah and his sons, 'I am now making my covenant with you and with your descendants, and with all living beings… I promise that never again will all living beings be destroyed by a flood… I am putting my bow in the clouds. It will be the sign of my covenant with the world.'

AT HOME

DID YOU KNOW?
Just like Noah, Abram and Sarai, we, too, are invited to place our trust in God, to have faith in God's plan for our lives and to believe that God will always keep his promises.

TIME TOGETHER

Chat Together
About times when it can be difficult to keep promises and to believe in promises that are made to us.

Read
Read together the passage from the Book of Genesis on page 8 of this book. It tells the story of God's promise to Abram and his wife Sarai, and of how Abram responded.

Invitation to Pray
God our Father, Creator of all life, help us to trust in you and to stay faithful to our promise to live as your people, a people of love. We ask this through Jesus Christ our Lord. Amen.

Be Prepared
Be prepared to consider carefully the promises you make to God and to others, and to keep those promises as best as you can.

Theme 1: God | Lesson 2: God's Promise to Abram

IN SCHOOL

THIS WEEK IN SCHOOL

You are invited to think about:
- God's covenant with Abraham and his wife Sarah
- Giving thanks to God for your Christian name, your baptismal name and your family name
- Sharing some ways in which you can show respect for your own name and others' names

THEME 1: GOD | LESSON 3

God's Covenant with Abraham

ABOUT NAMES

Over time, Abram's faith and trust in God deepened. To mark this growing relationship between God and Abram and to signal a new chapter in that relationship, God asked Abram (a name that means 'high father') to become Abraham (a name that means 'Father of the people'). God also asked Sarai (a name that means 'my princess') to change her name to Sarah (which means 'lady or noblewoman'). This change of name marked the couple's stronger commitment to their covenant with God – a commitment that involved leaving their old life behind. Giving the couple new names was God's way of showing that he had chosen them to play a special role in his plan for all people and all creation.

- Check out the original names of the following popes: St John Paul II, St John XXIII and Pope Francis.
- Can you name the occasion during which people choose a name to celebrate the beginning of their membership of the Christian community, the Church?
- Can you think of any other times when someone might choose a new name for themselves?

Pope Francis

St John XXIII

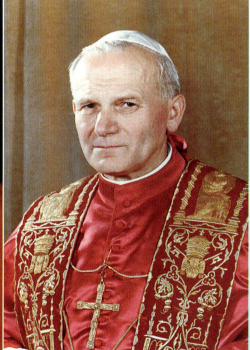

St John Paul II

IN SCHOOL

This passage from the Book of Genesis tells the story of God's covenant with Abraham and Sarah:

> **God's Covenant with Abraham (Genesis 17:1-8, 15-22)**
>
> When Abram was ninety-nine years old, the Lord appeared to him and said, 'I am the Almighty God. Obey me and always do what is right. I will make my covenant with you and give you many descendants.' Abram bowed down with his face touching the ground, and God said, 'I make this covenant with you: I promise that you will be the ancestor of many nations. Your name will no longer be Abram, but Abraham… I will give you many descendants, and some of them will be kings…
>
> 'I will be your God and the God of your descendants… The whole land of Canaan will belong to your descendants forever, and I will be their God.'
>
> God said to Abraham, 'You must no longer call your wife Sarai; from now on her name is Sarah. I will bless her, and I will give you a son by her. I will bless her, and she will become the mother of nations, and there will be kings among her descendants.'
>
> Abraham bowed down with his face touching the ground, but he began to laugh when he thought, 'Can a man have a child when he is a hundred years old? Can Sarah have a child at ninety?'…
>
> But God said, 'No. Your wife Sarah will bear you a son and you will name him Isaac. I will keep my covenant with him and with his descendants forever. It is an everlasting covenant.'

FOR MEMORISATION

'I will be your God and the God of your descendants.' (Genesis 17:7)

DISCUSS
- In pairs, discuss whether you feel that the names 'Abraham' and 'Sarah' were suitable names for them. Why or why not?
- Abraham and Sarah had a son and they named him Isaac. This name means 'laughter'. Do you thnk this was a suitable name for their son? Why or why not?

Theme 1: God | Lesson 3: God's Covenant with Abraham

AT HOME

DID YOU KNOW?

Today Abraham is recognised as the father of the Jewish people, father of the prophets of Islam and father in faith of Christians.

TIME TOGETHER

Chat Together

About the artwork in your child's Religious Education journal.

Talk about the name for God from the Old Testament that you like best, and why you like it.

Tell your child how you chose his/her name and what meaning is associated with the name.

Talk about what the advice that is given in 'St Teresa's Bookmark' means for you.

Invitation to Pray

God our Father, Creator of all life, you have called us by our names and you love us because of who we are. Help us never to forget your generous love for each one of us. We ask this through Jesus Christ our Lord. Amen.

Be Curious

Be curious to discover the meaning of your family name and your family crest. This may help to give you a clearer sense of how unique and special you are.

THIS WEEK

The children have been learning about the challenge that God presented to Abram and Sarai. God asked them to leave behind their old familiar life and enter into new and unfamiliar experiences. This challenge demanded great faith and trust on the part of Abram and Sarai. God changed Abram's name to Abraham to mark his becoming a leader of God's people. God also changed Sarai's name to Sarah. God promised Abraham and Sarah the gift of a son, Isaac, and many descendants. God's covenant with Abraham and his descendants was an everlasting covenant.

In the prayer 'St Teresa's Bookmark', the great Spanish saint Teresa of Ávila reminds us that neither the good things we experience in this life, nor the bad ones, last forever. God is always with us and God is all we need. Read 'St Teresa's Bookmark' together.

St Teresa's Bookmark

Let nothing disturb you,
Let nothing frighten you,
All things are passing;
God only is changeless.
Patience gains all things.
Who has God wants nothing.
God alone suffices.

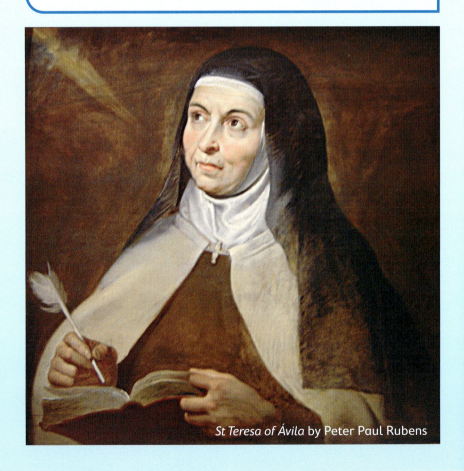

St Teresa of Ávila by Peter Paul Rubens

THEME 2: THE BIBLE | LESSON 1

The Bible, Our Sacred Scripture

ABOUT PRECIOUS THINGS

One of the most precious things to people of faith is their Sacred Scripture. The Bible is the Sacred Scripture of Christians. The people who wrote the Bible were inspired by the Holy Spirit.

The Bible is divided into two main sections: the Old Testament, which was written before the birth of Jesus, and the New Testament, which is about the life of Jesus and his followers. The New Testament contains the four Gospels, which were written by the Evangelists: Matthew, Mark, Luke and John. This section of the Bible describes the life, death, Resurrection and Ascension of Jesus Christ. The later books in the New Testament give an account of the lives of the disciples who founded the first Christian communities after Jesus returned to his Father in heaven. Christians have always had respect and reverence for this holy book.

- Think about your favourite story from the Old Testament. Why did you choose this story? What does it teach you about God?
- Think about your favourite story from the New Testament. Why did you choose this story? What does it teach you about God?

Prayer on Opening the Bible

Bless me, O God, so that
In opening this Bible
I may open my mind and my heart
To your Word.
May it nourish me
As it nourished Jesus. Amen.

Prayer on Closing the Bible

Bless me, O God,
So that in closing this Bible
I may enclose your Word
In my heart and in my mind
As Jesus enclosed it in his. Amen.

IN SCHOOL

THIS WEEK IN SCHOOL

You are invited to think about:
- Your favourite stories in the Old Testament and the New Testament
- Having an imaginary conversation with your chosen Evangelist
- Giving thanks to God for the gift of Sacred Scripture to teach us about him and his plan for all creation

KEY WORDS

Testament: The word 'testament' means 'covenant'. The two main parts of the Bible are the Old Testament and the New Testament.

New Testament: The part of the Bible that focuses on the life and teachings of Jesus. It contains the four Gospels.

Gospel: The word 'gospel' means 'good news'. The Good News for Christians is that God loves us and he sent his Son, Jesus, to show us how much he loves us. The word is also used to name the first four books in the New Testament, which were written by the Evangelists.

Evangelists: The name given to the four authors of the Gospels: Matthew, Mark, Luke and John.

Theme 2: The Bible | Lesson 1: The Bible, Our Sacred Scripture

IN SCHOOL

Book of Kells, folio 27v

ABOUT THE WORD
Jesus is called the Word of God. St John's Gospel tells us that before there was anything, Jesus (the Word) was present with God. Here is what John says about 'the Word':

> **The Word of Life (John 1:1-5)**
> In the beginning the Word already existed; the Word was with God, and the Word was God. From the very beginning the Word was with God. Through him God made all things; not one thing in all creation was made without him. The Word was the source of life, and this life brought light to people. The light shines in the darkness, and the darkness has never put it out.

DISCUSS
- Talk about why 'the Word' might be a good title for Jesus.

FOR MEMORISATION
There are four Gospels in the New Testament. They are the Gospel according to Matthew, the Gospel according to Mark, the Gospel according to Luke and the Gospel according to John.

Symbols of the Evangelists
The four symbols that are commonly used to represent the Evangelists were inspired by a vision that the great Old Testament prophet Ezekiel received from God.
- Matthew is represented by a winged man/angel.
- Mark is represented by a winged lion.
- Luke is represented by a winged calf.
- John is represented by an eagle.

ACTIVITY
Imagine you met one of the four Evangelists. Find a partner and act out the conversation. Here are some questions to get you started:
- Why did you decide to write about Jesus of Nazareth?
- What was it about Jesus that inspired you?
- What is the most important thing you want people to understand when they read your Gospel?

AT HOME

The Bible is a library of books written by people who were inspired by the Holy Spirit. It is divided into two main sections: the Old Testament and the New Testament. The first four books of the New Testament are the Gospels, which are central to our understanding of Jesus. Christians have always treated the Bible with great honour and respect, as shown in the exquisite copies of the Gospels presented in the Book of Durrow and the Book of Kells.

Read the reflection 'Imagine' together.

Imagine
Imagine a scribe
Holding paper in place
And the sweep of his pen
As he captures a space.
In the round of an 'O'
Or the curve of a 'C'
And the time he will spend
Inking leaves on a tree.
So the words of the Gospel
Will shimmer with light
And for hundreds of years
Will bring joy and delight.

AT HOME

DID YOU KNOW?
The last book in the New Testament is called the Book of Revelation.

TIME TOGETHER

Chat Together
You might like to visit your local library or go online at home to view images of folios (pages) in the Book of Kells. Talk about your favourite pages. Share opinions on why you think the Bible is treated with such honour and respect.

Invitation to Pray
God Our Creator, thank you for giving us your Word in the Bible. Help us always to listen to your Word and to hear what it is saying to us for our lives. Amen.

Be Prepared
Be prepared to listen carefully the next time you hear the Word of God being read in church.

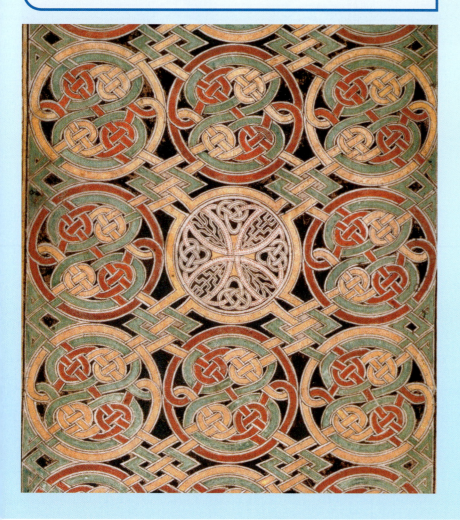

Book of Durrow, detail from folio 85v

Theme 2: The Bible | Lesson 1: The Bible, Our Sacred Scripture

IN SCHOOL

THIS WEEK IN SCHOOL

You are invited to think about:
- Giving thanks to God for the gift of Sacred Scripture to guide us through life
- Ways in which you can share the Good News that Jesus gave us in the New Testament

KEY WORDS

Acts of the Apostles: Title of the book that comes after the four Gospels in the New Testament. It describes the words and actions of some of the earliest followers of Jesus.

Letters or Epistles: Books in the New Testament that come after the Acts of the Apostles. They were written by the first Church leaders to teach and guide the early Christian communities.

Book of Revelation (Apocalypse): This is the final book in the New Testament. It is full of symbols and can be difficult to understand. It speaks about what will happen at the end of the world.

THEME 2: THE BIBLE | LESSON 2

The New Testament

ABOUT GUIDANCE
Every day we make choices and decisions. Sometimes life can get confusing and it can be difficult to choose the best thing to say or do in a given situation. The Bible is there to guide people of faith on how to live as Jesus did and as he asked his followers to do.

This passage from the Second Letter to Timothy tells us why we should read the Bible:

> **Scripture Teaches Us the Truth (2 Timothy 3:16—17)**
> All Scripture is inspired by God and is useful for teaching the truth, … correcting faults, and giving instruction for right living, so that the person who serves God may be fully qualified and equipped to do every kind of good deed.

- Do you agree with these words from Timothy's letter? Why or why not?
- Can you give an example of a passage from the New Testament that you think could help you to live as a follower of Jesus?

IN SCHOOL

ABOUT GOOD NEWS

Jesus came on earth to tell us the Good News of God's love for us. These are the words Jesus spoke before he began his mission of teaching the people about God and showing them how to live:

Good News (Luke 4:18)

'The Spirit of the Lord is upon me,
because he has chosen me to bring good news…'

DISCUSS

- In pairs or groups, recall what you know about the Good News that Jesus brought.
- In what different ways did Jesus share the Good News of God's love with the people he met? Give examples.
- Take turns to share how you can bring the Good News of God's love to the people whom you will meet today.

Read these words from St Paul's first letter to the people of Corinth, which teach about the meaning of love:

Love (1 Corinthians 13:4-7)

Love is patient and kind; it is not jealous or conceited or proud; love is not ill-mannered or selfish or irritable; love does not keep a record of wrongs; love is not happy with evil, but is happy with the truth. Love never gives up; and its faith, hope and patience never fail.

FOR MEMORISATION

Love is patient and kind.
(1 Corinthians 13:4)

ACTIVITY

- Read the above passage about the meaning of love again, this time quietly saying your name every time you see the word *love*.
- Are all these statements true for you at this time in your life? Or do you sometimes find it difficult to be loving?
- You might like to ask God to help you to see how you can be more loving towards others.

Theme 2: The Bible | Lesson 2: The New Testament

AT HOME

DID YOU KNOW?

The Bible is sacred to people of the Christian faith. They believe that the person of Jesus is central to their faith.

TIME TOGETHER

Chat Together
Share your favourite story about Jesus. Look at and respond to the images below. In what ways do they depict love?

Read
Read together the short passage from the first letter of St Paul on the previous page, in which he teaches about the meaning of love.

Invitation to Pray
Loving God, Creator of life and of love, help us to choose love in all that we think, say and do. We ask this through Jesus Christ our Lord. Amen.

Be Loving
Be willing to show love in a new way to someone in your family whom you find it difficult to get along with at the moment.

THIS WEEK
The children learned that the person of Jesus and his message of love are central to the twenty-seven books in the New Testament. The New Testament contains the four Gospels, the Acts of the Apostles, the Letters (or Epistles) and the Book of Revelation. The central focus of the New Testament is the life and teachings of Jesus and of his first followers in the early Church.

Below are some words of advice based on the Letter of St James. Do you think this is good advice? Why or why not?

Advice from St James
Pray for wisdom.
Be quick to listen but slow to speak.
Be friendly.
Be peaceful.
Do not criticise one another.
Do not complain.

18   Grow in Love | Fourth Class/Primary 6

THEME 3: JESUS | LESSON 1

The Parable of the Mustard Seed

ABOUT GROWING

All living things grow and change. Consider a younger member of your family, an animal or pet that you are familiar with or a seed that you planted. Think about how the person, animal or seed has grown and developed over time.

Talk to the child who is sitting nearest to you about something in your life that started off in a small way but grew to become more significant and meaningful as time passed. For example, someone might have given you a musical instrument when you were younger, and now you are able to play it. Or you might have enjoyed helping an older member of your family in the kitchen or in the garden, and now you love cooking or gardening.

IN SCHOOL

THIS WEEK IN SCHOOL

You are invited to think about:
- The Parable of the Mustard Seed
- How small things can change and develop and become more significant
- Thanking God for giving us the ability to make the Kingdom of God grow here on earth

KEY WORDS

Parable: A simple, easy-to-understand story that is used to teach something important. Jesus often told parables to teach people about the Kingdom of God.

Kingdom of God: It is also called the Kingdom of Heaven. This does not refer to a specific location or to any physical place. Instead, it refers to the type of world that we create when we live according to the values that Jesus taught. The Kingdom of God exists wherever people live together in a community of justice, peace and love.

Theme 3: Jesus | Lesson 1: The Parable of the Mustard Seed

IN SCHOOL

ABOUT THE KINGDOM OF GOD

Jesus told the people a parable about a mustard seed. He wanted to help them to understand that, just as a tiny mustard seed grows to become a tree, the Kingdom of God grows out of the words and actions of all those who live according to his teachings.

FOR MEMORISATION

The Kingdom of God is like a mustard seed that grows and becomes a tree.

The Parable of the Mustard Seed (Luke 13:18–19)

Jesus asked, 'What is the Kingdom of God like? What shall I compare it with? It is like this. A man takes a mustard seed and plants it in his field. The plant grows and becomes a tree, and the birds make their nests in its branches.'

DISCUSS

- Do you think the example of a mustard seed growing from a small seed into a large tree was a good one to use to help people understand something about the Kingdom of God? Why or why not?
- What other examples might help people to understand what the Kingdom of God is and how it comes about?
- What have you learned from the Parable of the Mustard Seed about how you personally can contribute to building the Kingdom of God?

THIS WEEK
The children have been learning that, in God's view of the world, those things that at first glance might appear insignificant are sometimes the most significant of all. Jesus compared the Kingdom of God to a mustard seed, the tiniest of seeds that grows to become a really big tree.

Read the poem 'The Mustard Seed' together.

The Mustard Seed

It was winter.
The little seeds lay in the ground,
All comfy and cosy
And coloured and round,
And they chatted together
Deep down from the snow.
How high they would sprout
When the time came to grow!
'I'll be off like a shot,'
Said the daisy with pride,
'And I'll smile at the sun
While you other seeds hide.'
Then the dandelion sniggered,
'You'll be away fast,
But we all know that daisies
Are no good to last.
I'll grow in the springtime,
My stem long and fat,
And I'll have for the rain
A most elegant hat.'
But the mustard seed sat there,
The smallest of all,
And waited with patience
For spring's gentle call.
Then he reached up a shoot
And started to climb
From a sprout, to a twig,
To a tree, and in time
To the greatest of trees
Standing mighty and tall,
With its branches held wide
As a welcome to all.
And far down below
All the plants were agreed
That God had done best
With a small little seed.

AT HOME

DID YOU KNOW?
The mustard tree grows wild in North Africa, the Middle East and around the Mediterranean.

TIME TOGETHER

Chat Together
About the poem 'The Mustard Seed'. What are your favourite lines? Talk to your child about how he or she has grown since they were born. If possible, look at photographs showing different stages of their growth. Next time you pass a health food store, you might like to see if they sell mustard seeds. Check out how tiny these seeds are.

Invitation to Pray
Loving God, guide us to be more like Jesus with each passing day, so that we can help to build your kingdom in our world and in our hearts. We ask this through Jesus Christ our Lord. Amen.

Be Thankful
Be thankful for the ability God has given you to help build his kingdom on earth.

Theme 3: Jesus | Lesson 1: The Parable of the Mustard Seed

IN SCHOOL

THIS WEEK IN SCHOOL

You are invited to think about:
- The Parable of the Good Samaritan
- What it means to be a good neighbour
- The advice of St Francis of Assisi: 'Preach the Gospel at all times, but only use words when necessary.'
- Giving thanks to God for the 'Good Samaritans' who have helped you throughout your own life

KEY WORDS

Neighbour: For Christians, our neighbour means all people. When Jesus said that we must love our neighbour, he was challenging us to treat all people equally and with loving kindness.

Priest (in the time of Jesus): Leader of worship in the Temple.

Levites: Men from the tribe of Levi who helped the priests with their work in the Temple.

Jews: Name for God's Chosen People, the descendants of Abraham.

Samaritans: People from Samaria, the capital of the northern Kingdom of Israel.

THEME 3: JESUS | LESSON 2

The Parable of the Good Samaritan

ABOUT GOOD NEIGHBOURS

Jesus told us that we must love God and love our neighbour. For Christians, our neighbour means everyone – even people whom we find difficult to like. Being a good neighbour means treating other people with respect and kindness – as we like to be treated.

Sometimes we are tempted to put ourselves first and not be good neighbours. Recall the story 'The Sports Day'. Who was the good neighbour in that story? Can you think of a time in your own life when you saw people acting as good neighbours?

THE GOOD SAMARITAN

Jesus told a parable about a good Samaritan. Samaritans were people who lived in Samaria, the capital of the northern Kingdom of Israel in the time of Jesus. The Samaritans' neighbours, the Jews, looked down on them and didn't like to have anything to do with them. Jews regarded Samaritans as inferior to them in all things. A Jew would even cross the road rather than walk on the same side as a Samaritan.

> **The Parable of the Good Samaritan (Luke 10:25-37)**
>
> A teacher of the Law came up and tried to trap Jesus. 'Teacher,' he asked, 'what must I do to receive eternal life?'
>
> Jesus answered him, 'What do the Scriptures say? How do you interpret them?'
>
> The man answered, ' "Love the Lord your God with all your heart, with all your soul, with all your strength, and with all your mind"; and "Love your neighbour as you love yourself." '
>
> 'You are right,' Jesus replied; 'do this and you will live.'
>
> But the teacher of the Law wanted to justify himself, so he asked Jesus, 'Who is my neighbour?'
>
> Jesus answered, 'There was once a man who was going down from Jerusalem to Jericho when robbers attacked him, stripped him, and beat him up, leaving him half dead. It so happened that a priest was going down that road; but when he saw the man, he walked on by on the other side. But a Samaritan who was travelling that way came upon the man, and when he saw him, his heart was filled with pity. He went over to him, poured oil and wine on his wounds and bandaged them; then he put the

IN SCHOOL

The Good Samaritan by Vincent Van Gogh (after Delacroix) (1890)

man on his own animal and took him to an inn, where he took care of him. The next day he took out two silver coins and gave them to the innkeeper. "Take care of him," he told the innkeeper, "and when I come back this way, I will pay whatever else you spend on him." '

And Jesus concluded, 'In your opinion, which one of these three acted like a neighbour towards the man attacked by the robbers?'

The teacher of the Law answered, 'The one who was kind to him.'

Jesus replied, 'You go, then, and do the same.'

DISCUSS
- Would the people who were listening have been surprised by anything in this parable? What would they have been surprised to hear?
- Why do you think Jesus told this parable?
- What does this parable tell you about how you should live as a Christian in the world today?
- Can you recall a time when you acted like a 'Good Samaritan'? What did you do? Whom did you help?

ACTIVITY
Take a little time to think about what St Francis of Assisi meant when he said: 'Preach the Gospel at all times, but only use words when necessary.'
- In your Religious Education journal record some ways you shared the Good News with others without using words.

FOR MEMORISATION

'Love the Lord your God with all your heart, with all your soul, with all your strength, and with all your mind' and 'love your neighbour as you love yourself.' (Luke 10:27)

We show our love for our neighbours by respecting them and their property, by being truthful and honest, by sharing with them and by wishing them well.

Theme 3: Jesus | Lesson 2: The Parable of the Good Samaritan

AT HOME

DID YOU KNOW?

Jesus challenges us to look beyond tribes and territory and to reach out in love and friendship to all people.

TIME TOGETHER

Chat Together
About the message that the poet is trying to communicate in this poem? Do you agree with this message? Why or why not? Talk about labelling others. Is it easy to develop the habit of judging others? Why or why not? Share ideas about how you can avoid this habit.

Invitation to Pray
Jesus our teacher, you taught us that loving God and loving our neighbour are inseparable. Help us in our daily lives to be 'Good Samaritans', to act out of love towards everyone we meet. Amen.

Be Grateful
Be grateful to God for the 'Good Samaritans' in your life.

THIS WEEK
The children heard the Parable of the Good Samaritan. The least likely person in the story responded to the needs of the man who was injured. Jesus wanted people to be very careful about how they judge others. As followers of Jesus, we are challenged to treat all people equally and with loving kindness. We are to look on all people as our neighbours – even those who are different from us or those whom we may find it difficult to like.

Read the poem 'Love of God and Neighbour' together.

Love of God and Neighbour

Like the day and its light,
The wind and its blow,
The word and its meaning,
The bread and its dough,
The night and its darkness,
The noun and its name,
The wool and its softness,
The twin and its same,
The water and its wetness,
The heart and its beat,
The smile and its face,
The flame and its heat,
The road and its journey,
The job and its labour,

There's no 'loving God'
 Without 'loving neighbour'.

THEME 3: JESUS | LESSON 3

The Parable of the Lost Coin

ABOUT LOSING SOMETHING PRECIOUS

Some things are more precious than others. What is precious to you may not be precious to someone else.
- Do you have something that is very precious to you?
- Why is it precious?
- Who gave it to you?
- Could it be easily replaced? Why or why not?

Recall the story about Selina and Bonzo.
- How did Selina feel when she discovered that Bonzo was missing? What did she do?
- What would you do if you lost your precious item?

IN SCHOOL

THIS WEEK IN SCHOOL

You are invited to think about:
- The Parable of the Lost Coin
- What it is like to feel lost
- The Parable of the Lost Sheep
- Praying to St Anthony when you have lost something
- Giving thanks to God who searches for us when we are lost and who is overjoyed when we are found and return to him

KEY WORDS

Coin: The coins in the Parable of the Lost Coin were probably drachmas. It was most unusual for poor people to have money in those days. Therefore, the lost coin would have been of great value to the woman.

Sin: Anything we do or say that breaks Jesus' law of love and weakens or destroys our friendship with God.

Repent: To be sorry for our sins and to seek God's forgiveness.

Selina and Bonzo

Theme 3: Jesus | Lesson 3: The Parable of the Lost Coin

IN SCHOOL

One day Jesus told the people a parable about a lost coin. Jesus was helping the people to understand the Kingdom of God and their place in it.

The Parable of the Lost Coin (Luke 15:8-10)

'Suppose a woman who has ten silver coins loses one of them – what does she do? She lights a lamp, sweeps her house, and looks carefully everywhere until she finds it. When she finds it, she calls her friends and neighbours together, and says to them, "I am so happy I found the coin I lost. Let us celebrate!" In the same way, I tell you, the angels of God rejoice over one sinner who repents.'

FOR MEMORISATION

'… the angels of God rejoice over one sinner who repents.' (Luke 15:10)

DISCUSS

- What did the woman do when she discovered that her coin was lost?
- How did the woman react when she found her lost coin? What does that tell you about how precious the coin was to her?
- Did you ever celebrate when you found something you had lost? Describe what happened.

ABOUT FEELING LOST

Sometimes people can feel lost. They can feel out of touch or disconnected from other people or just unhappy and alone in themselves. In groups, talk about times when you have felt like this. Do you know anyone who might be feeling lost and alone at this time? What can you do to help them?

ACTIVITY

- In your Religious Education journal, record a time when you felt lost and then you experienced the joy of being found again. Write a short prayer about that experience.

AT HOME

DID YOU KNOW?
The coins in the Parable of the Lost Coin were drachmas and, in the time of Jesus, each one would have been worth the equivalent of a day's wage for a worker.

TIME TOGETHER

Chat Together
Ask your child to tell you about the woman in the parable who lost the coin, and what she did when she found it. See if your child knows what Jesus was trying to teach through this parable.

Invitation to Pray
St Anthony, you received from God the special power to help people to find things that are lost. Help me to find _____ which I have lost. Help me never to lose the most important thing of all, which is my friendship with God. Amen.

Be Joyful
Be full of joy, knowing that God is always present in your life.

THIS WEEK
The children heard the Parable of the Lost Coin. They explored how sometimes people can feel lost inside. We feel lost inside when we do things that separate us from the people who love us and from God. Jesus used the Parable of the Lost Coin to teach us that God is always overjoyed when those who are lost from his love decide to return to him.

St Anthony's Lost Book
Many people ask St Anthony to help them to find things that are lost. The reason people ask for St Anthony's help to find things is linked to a particular event in his life. Anthony was a preacher and he owned a book of psalms containing his personal notes which he used to teach his students. One day Anthony noticed his precious book was missing. He prayed that the book would be found. The thief had a change of heart and he returned the book to Anthony. Today, St Anthony's book is said to be kept in the Franciscan Friary in Bologna, Italy.

DISCUSS
- St Anthony prayed for the safe return of his precious book. When do you pray?
- The thief had a change of heart and he returned the book to Anthony. Have you ever done something wrong but then changed your mind and did the right thing? What caused you to change your mind? How did you feel then?

Theme 3: Jesus | Lesson 3: The Parable of the Lost Coin

IN SCHOOL

THIS WEEK IN SCHOOL

You are invited to think about:
- The Parable of the Widow and the Judge
- An imaginary conversation between yourself and the widow in the parable
- Giving thanks to God for Jesus, who taught us through parables how to build the Kingdom of God

KEY WORDS

Widow: A woman whose husband has died. In the time of Jesus widows had very little money or power.

Faith: Belief.

Serenity: The feeling of being calm and peaceful.

THEME 3: JESUS | LESSON 4

The Parable of the Widow and the Judge

ABOUT PERSISTENCE AND PATIENCE

Maybe you can remember learning to skip, to ride a bike or to play an instrument. Recall a time when you had to be persistent and very patient with yourself so that you could achieve your goal. What or who helped you to stay strong and positive until you completed your task or challenge?

Jesus tells us that we need to be persistent and patient in our prayers. God always responds to our prayers, but not always in the way we might expect or in the timeframe we desire.

FIND OUT

With a partner, find out about people in history who peacefully persisted in campaigning for justice and improvements for their own lives and the lives of others, for example, Rosa Parks and Martin Luther King.

DISCUSS

- Recall the fable about the crow and the pitcher. What did you learn from that fable?
- Why is it important to be persistent and patient when we are trying to achieve something important?
- What can happen when we give up easily or lack patience?

The Widow and the Judge by John F. Shaw (c. 1890)

LOOK AND RESPOND

- What do you see in the painting?
- What do you notice about the judge? How do you think he is feeling?
- What do you notice about the widow? How do you think she feels?
- What about the onlookers? What might they be thinking?

IN SCHOOL

Jesus told his disciples this parable:

> **The Parable of the Widow and the Judge (Luke 18:1-8)**
>
> 'In a certain town there was a judge who neither feared God nor respected people. And there was a widow in that same town who kept coming to him and pleading for her rights, saying, 'Help me against my opponent!' For a long time the judge refused to act, but at last he said to himself, "Even though I don't fear God or respect people, yet because of all the trouble this widow is giving me, I will see to it that she gets her rights. If I don't, she will keep on coming and finally wear me out!" '
>
> And the Lord continued, 'Listen to what that corrupt judge said. Now, will God not judge in favour of his own people who cry to him day and night for help? Will he be slow to help them? I tell you, he will judge in their favour and do it quickly. But will the Son of Man find faith on earth when he comes?'

DISCUSS
- Why did the judge give in to the widow?
- Share examples of times when your persistence and patience achieved good results.
- Share examples of times when you gave in to someone else's need.

ACTIVITY
Imagine you are friends with the widow and you know about her dealings with the judge. Find a partner and act out the conversation. Here are some questions to get you started:
- Why did you go to the judge?
- How did the judge react?
- What did the judge decide to do in the end? Why do you think he made that decision?
- Do you feel you got justice?

RECORD
Complete the following two statements in your Religious Education journal. Then share them with a parent or guardian.
- Jesus told many parables to teach people about the Kingdom of God. My favourite parable is the one about the … I like this parable because …
- I have learned a lot from Jesus' parables about the Kingdom of God. I would describe the Kingdom of God as …

FOR MEMORISATION

How precious, O God, is your constant love! (Psalm 36:7)

Theme 3: Jesus | Lesson 4: The Parable of the Widow and the Judge

AT HOME

DID YOU KNOW?

God always responds to our prayers, but not always in the way we might expect or in the timeframe we desire.

TIME TOGETHER

Chat Together
About the advice the writer offers in the reflection 'Anyway'. Do you agree with this advice? Why or why not? Which piece of advice would you find hardest to take on board? Why?
Consider the qualities of persistence and patience. Who in your family best models these qualities for you? Which of these two do you find most difficult to put into practice?

Invitation to Pray
Loving God, help us to listen attentively to the parables that Jesus shared with us. We ask this through Jesus Christ our Lord. Amen.

Be Reflective
Take some time to think about the wisdom you have found for your own life in the parables of Jesus.

THIS WEEK
The children heard the Parable of the Widow and the Judge. The unjust judge responded to the persistent widow, who was seeking justice from him. Jesus tells us that we need to be persistent and patient when we pray. We also need to be persistent and patient in seeking what is good and just for ourselves and others.

Read the reflection 'Anyway' together.

> **Anyway**
>
> People are often unreasonable, irrational and self-centred. Forgive them anyway.
> If you are kind, people may accuse you of selfish, ulterior motives. Be kind anyway.
> If you are successful, you will win some unfaithful friends and some genuine enemies. Succeed anyway.
> If you are honest and sincere, people may deceive you. Be honest and sincere anyway.
> What you spend years creating, others could destroy overnight. Create anyway.
> If you find serenity and joy, some may be jealous. Be joyful anyway.
> The good you do today will often be forgotten. Do good anyway.
> Give the best you have, and it will never be enough. Give your best anyway…
> – Attributed to St. Teresa of Calcutta

THEME 4: ADVENT AND CHRISTMAS | LESSON 1

Zechariah and Elizabeth

ABOUT ADVENT

One of the most precious things we have in our lives is the gift of time. Advent is a special time in the Church calendar. It marks the beginning of the Liturgical Year and the four-week countdown to the feast of the Nativity, 25 December, when we remember and celebrate the birth of Jesus.

Advent is the time when we prepare for and look forward to reliving this great event. It is a time of prayer and hope, as we wait to welcome Christ once again into our hearts and into our lives. During Advent we remember, too, how Mary waited for the birth of her Son, Jesus, and how Elizabeth and Zechariah also waited for God's plan to unfold.

ZECHARIAH AND ELIZABETH RECEIVE GOOD NEWS

During the season of Advent we recall the elderly couple, Zechariah and Elizabeth, who waited patiently and hopefully for God's plan to unfold. Zechariah was a priest in the Temple and Elizabeth was Mary's cousin. They had no children. One day while Zechariah was burning incense at the altar, an angel appeared to him. Here is the story:

> **The Birth of John the Baptist is Announced (Luke 1:8, 11, 13-25)**
>
> One day Zechariah was doing his work as a priest in the Temple, taking his turn in the daily service… An angel of the Lord appeared to him… When Zechariah saw him, he was alarmed and felt afraid. But the angel said to him, 'Don't be afraid, Zechariah! God has heard your prayer, and your wife Elizabeth will bear you a son. You are to name him John. How glad and happy you will be, and how happy many others will be when he is born! John will be great in the Lord's sight… From his very birth he will be filled with the Holy Spirit, and he will bring back many of the people of Israel to the Lord their God. He will go ahead of the Lord, strong and mighty like the prophet Elijah. He will bring fathers and children together again; he will turn disobedient people back to the way of thinking of the righteous; he will get the Lord's people ready for him.'
>
> Zechariah said to the angel, 'How shall I know if this is so? I am an old man, and my wife is old also.'

IN SCHOOL

THIS WEEK IN SCHOOL

You are invited to think about:
- The story of Zechariah and Elizabeth
- Mary's response to Angel Gabriel
- An imaginary conversation between Zechariah and Mary
- Giving thanks to God for the gift of times of joy and good news

KEY WORDS

Liturgy: The public prayer of the Church.

Liturgical Year: Name for the cycle of seasons celebrated in the Church calendar.

Advent: The first season in the Liturgical Year. The word 'Advent' means 'coming'. The season of Advent marks the countdown of four weeks leading to the coming or birth of Jesus Christ.

Servant: A person who puts himself or herself at the service of another. In the Bible, a servant of God is someone who is totally committed to doing God's will by living a life of selfless love.

Theme 4: Advent and Christmas | Lesson 1: Zechariah and Elizabeth

IN SCHOOL

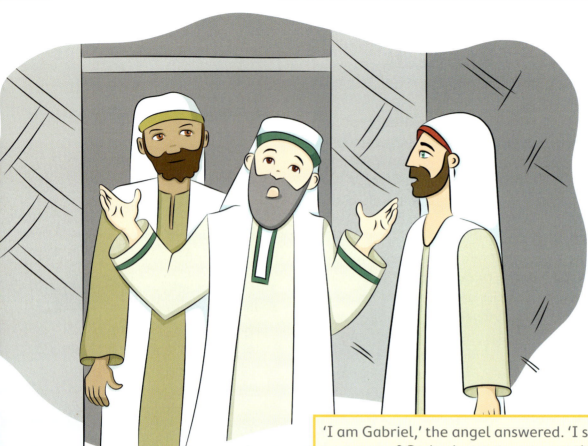

FOR MEMORISATION

'There is nothing that God cannot do.' (Luke 1:37)

'I am Gabriel,' the angel answered. 'I stand in the presence of God, who sent me to speak to you and tell you this good news. But you have not believed my message, which will come true at the right time. Because you have not believed, you will be unable to speak; you will remain silent until the day my promise to you comes true.'

In the meantime the people were waiting for Zechariah and wondered why he was spending such a long time in the Temple. When he came out, he could not speak to them, and so they knew that he had seen a vision in the Temple. Unable to say a word, he made signs to them with his hands …

Some time later [Elizabeth] became pregnant…

DISCUSS
- How do you think Zechariah would have communicated with Elizabeth when he went home that day?
- Six months later the angel Gabriel appeared to Mary. What message did Angel Gabriel give to Mary?

ACTIVITY
The angel told Mary that her cousin Elizabeth was also pregnant. So Mary went to visit Elizabeth.
- Imagine the conversation that might have taken place between Mary and Elizabeth's husband, Zechariah. With a partner, act out the conversation.

THIS WEEK
The children have been talking about Advent, the season when we prepare to remember the birth of Jesus and to celebrate his coming once again into our hearts. It is a time when we also look forward to the second coming of Christ at the end of time. The children have heard the story of Zechariah and Elizabeth, the elderly couple who prayed to the Lord that they would have a baby, and God answered their prayer. They have also recalled how Mary responded to God's call to be the mother of Jesus. Mary and Joseph and Elizabeth and Zechariah waited patiently for their sons to be born. These stories from Sacred Scripture remind us that God's will is only accomplished in God's time, and sometimes we, too, must wait!

Read the poem 'Christmas Eve' together.

Christmas Eve

On Christmas Eve my mother read
    The story once again
Of how the little child was born
    And of the Three Wise Men.

And how by following the Star
    They found Him where He lay,
And brought Him gifts; and that is why
    We keep our Christmas Day.

And when she read it all, I went
    And looked across the snow
And thought of Jesus coming
    As He did long ago.

I looked into the East, and saw
    A great star blazing bright;
There were three men upon the road
    All black against the light.

I thought I heard the angels sing
    Away upon the hill…
I held my breath … it seemed as if
    The whole great world were still.

It seemed to me the little Child
    Was being born again …
And very near … and THEN somehow
Was NOW … or NOW was THEN.

AT HOME

DID YOU KNOW?
There are two Zechariahs in the Bible: Zechariah the husband of Elizabeth, and the Old Testament prophet called Zechariah.

TIME TOGETHER

Chat Together
About the possibility of having an Advent wreath in your home during the Advent season.

Share
Share your happy memories of your child's birth or of a recent birth in your family. Imagine the excitement Elizabeth and Zechariah must have felt when they were told that they were going to have a baby. We remember the time Angel Gabriel appeared to Mary when we pray the *Angelus*. Imagine how Mary felt about giving birth to Jesus, the Son of God.

Invitation to Pray
Pray the *Angelus* together.

Be Still
When you hear the Angelus bell, allow happiness to fill your heart.

Theme 4: Advent and Christmas | Lesson 1: Zechariah and Elizabeth

IN SCHOOL

THIS WEEK IN SCHOOL

You are invited to think about:
- All the stories in the Bible that tell of the events surrounding the birth of Jesus
- Giving thanks to God for the gifts of joy and wisdom
- Ways in which you can be welcoming and of service to others

KEY WORDS

The Epiphany: This feast day is celebrated on the last day of the season of Christmas, 6 January. On this day we remember the visit of the wise men to the stable in Bethlehem.

Holy Days of Obligation: In Ireland, there are five Holy Days of Obligation:
- The Nativity of the Lord (25 December)
- St Patrick's Day (17 March)
- The Assumption of the Blessed Virgin Mary (15 August)
- All Saints' Day (1 November)
- The Immaculate Conception (8 December)

The Catholic Church asks its members to go to Mass on Holy Days of Obligation.

Martyr: Someone who is put to death for their faith.

THEME 4: ADVENT AND CHRISTMAS | LESSON 2

The Epiphany

ABOUT THE LIGHT OF CHRIST

Throughout the dark days of winter we wait in hope for the light that Christ gives us at Christmas. Our candle-flames burn brightly on the Advent wreath, the shiny tinsel and decorations sparkle on the Christmas trees, and we remember the stunning light of the star that guided the wise men to Bethlehem. There they experienced the pure light of the love of God in the birth of his Son, Jesus.

Many people down the ages have sought to bring the light of Christ into the lives of others. One such person was St Lucy.

The Story of St Lucy

St Lucy (also known as St Lucia) (c. 283-304) was born in Syracuse in Sicily, an island off the southern coast of Italy. That was in the time of the Roman Empire, when life was difficult and dangerous for Christians. Roman soldiers patrolled the streets ready to torture, arrest or kill anyone suspected of being a Christian.

Lucy was a devout Christian and she got great courage from her faith. She was seen bringing bread to the hungry Christians who had come to worship God in secret underground caves, called catacombs. Lucy came to the attention of the authorities, but she refused to deny her Christian beliefs, and so she was put to death – martyred for her faith.

However, this brave woman was not forgotten. Some time after her death Lucy was named a saint. Many people in different countries around the world still remember St Lucy as a symbol of Christ's light in a time of fear and darkness. She is the patron saint of eyes, the body's source of light. People with eye problems often ask St Lucy to help them.

St Lucy by Artemisia Gentileschi (c. 1642–4)

ABOUT THE EPIPHANY

The Church remembers the visit of the three wise men to the newborn baby Jesus in the stable in Bethlehem on the feast of the Epiphany, which we celebrate on 6 January. The three men had followed a star which led them to the stable. They recognised that Jesus was the Son of God and they worshipped him. Here is the story from the Gospel according to Matthew:

> **Visitors from the East (Matthew 2:1-12)**
>
> Jesus was born in the town of Bethlehem in Judea, during the time when Herod was king. Soon afterward, some men who studied the stars came from the East to Jerusalem and asked, 'Where is the baby born to be king of the Jews? We saw his star when it came up in the east, and we have come to worship him.'
>
> When King Herod heard about this, he was very upset, and so was everyone else in Jerusalem. He called together all the chief priests and the teachers of the Law and asked them, 'Where will the Messiah be born?'
>
> 'In the town of Bethlehem in Judea,' they answered. 'For this is what the prophet wrote:
> "Bethlehem in the land of Judah,
> you are by no means the least of
> the leading cities of Judah;
> for from you will come a leader
> who will guide my people Israel." '
>
> So Herod called the visitors from the East to a secret meeting and found out from them the exact time the star had appeared. Then he sent them to Bethlehem with these instructions: 'Go and make a careful search for the child; and when you find him, let me know, so that I too may go and worship him.'
>
> And so they left, and on their way they saw the same star they had seen in the East. When they saw it, how happy they were, what joy was theirs! It went ahead of them until it stopped over the place where the child was. They went into the house, and when they saw the child with his mother Mary, they knelt down and worshipped him. They brought out their gifts of gold, frankincense and myrrh, and presented them to him.
>
> Then they returned to their country by another road, since God had warned them in a dream not to go back to Herod.

FOR MEMORISATION

… when they saw the child with his mother Mary, they knelt down and worshipped him. (Matthew 2:11)

Theme 4: Advent and Christmas | Lesson 2: The Epiphany

AT HOME

DID YOU KNOW?

The word 'January' comes from a Latin word meaning 'doorway'. It is an old custom to bless doorways at the time of the Epiphany (6 January) – as a reminder to welcome new people and guests during the year ahead. Some people also write the date and the letters CMB above their door. These are the first letters of the traditional names for the three wise men: Caspar, Melchior and Balthasar.

TIME TOGETHER

Chat Together
About the feast of the Epiphany and the tradition of Nollaig na mBan.
Share your favourite Christmas stories from the Bible.

Remember
That Mary and Joseph were strangers in Bethlehem. They were far away from their home town of Nazareth. Talk about the importance of welcoming new people and guests into our homes and into our country.

Invitation to Pray
Loving God, fill us with the same happiness and joy that the three wise men felt when they recognised the baby Jesus as the Son of God. We ask this through Jesus Christ our Lord. Amen.

Be of Service
Be willing to allow your child to be of service to you on Nollaig na mBan.

THIS WEEK
The children heard the story of the Three Wise Men and how they followed the star that led them to the place where Jesus was born. The men recognised Jesus as the Son of God and they knelt down before him and worshipped him.

The children also heard the story of St Lucy, who brought the light of Christ into people's lives through her acts of love and generosity. Today, Jesus helps us, too, to bring the light of his love into the world.

Pray this reflection together:

> Loving God, fill our hearts with kindness. Teach us to give a joyful welcome to everyone. Fill us with true wisdom so that we may always seek to follow the light of Christ and be like Jesus – today, tomorrow and throughout the New Year ahead. We ask this through Jesus Christ our Lord. Amen.

THEME 5: TRUSTING GOD | LESSON 1

Trust in God

ABOUT GIVING UP
Recall the story 'The Jigsaw'. Think about how Ronan's and Niamh's dad encouraged them to persevere with the jigsaw puzzle when they wanted to give up.
- Did you ever feel like giving up on something that you had started? Did you give up or did you persevere?
- What made you decide to either give up or keep going? How did you feel afterwards?

ABOUT PROMISES
People make promises all the time. Some people are good at making promises and at keeping their promises. Others make promises and then forget all about them.
- Did you ever promise, for example, that you would clean your room, wash the dishes, take the dog for a walk – and then forget to do what you had promised?
- When did you promise to do something and then actually do it? How did you feel afterwards?
- What helps you to keep your promises?

ACTIVITY
- Think about a promise, big or small, that you will make to your parents or guardians. In your Religious Education journal write a short letter to God asking him to help you keep that promise.

IN SCHOOL

THIS WEEK IN SCHOOL
You are invited to think about:
- Moses' response to God's call
- Your response to God's call
- Keeping promises in the Lenten season
- Ways you show trust in God

KEY WORDS
Sacrifice: When someone gives up something they like for the good of someone else.

Hebrews: The Jewish people of ancient Israel, the Israelites, were also known as Hebrews. They were God's Chosen People.

Locust: A type of grasshopper.

Advocate: A person who pleads for a cause on behalf of another.

Moses and Aaron Visit the King of Egypt
God asked Moses to go to the king, or pharaoh, of Egypt and ask him to free the Israelites from their slavery in his country. Moses agreed to do as God asked. Aaron, Moses' brother, went with him. They asked the king to allow the people to go into the desert for three days to worship God. The king refused their request. Instead, he made life even more difficult for the Israelites.

Moses didn't give up, but kept on trying to persuade the king. God promised Moses that he would send a plague of locusts to the land of Egypt if the king continued to refuse to free the people. Moses warned the king of what God had said. Now read the account of what happened as it is told in chapter 10 of the Book of Exodus.

Theme 5: Trusting God | Lesson 1: Trust in God

IN SCHOOL

So Moses and Aaron went to the king and said to him, 'The Lord, the God of the Hebrews, says, ..."if you keep on refusing, then I will bring locusts into your country tomorrow. There will be so many that they will completely cover the ground. They will eat everything... They will fill your palaces and the houses of all your officials and all your people..." ' Then Moses turned and left...

Then the Lord said to Moses, 'Raise your hand over the land of Egypt to bring the locusts...' So Moses raised his stick... The locusts came in swarms and settled over the whole country...

Then the king hurriedly called Moses and Aaron and said, 'I have sinned against the Lord your God and against you. Now forgive my sin ... and pray to the Lord your God to take away this fatal punishment from me.' Moses left the king and prayed to the Lord. And the Lord changed the east wind into a very strong west wind, which picked up the locusts and blew them into the Gulf of Suez. Not one locust was left in all of Egypt. But ... he did not let the Israelites go.

The swarm of locusts was the first of ten plagues that God sent to punish the king for refusing to let the Israelites leave Egypt. God sent nine more plagues before the Israelites eventually escaped into the desert with Moses.

God continued to talk to Moses as he led the people out of Egypt. God promised he would be with them all the way and he kept his promise. The Egyptian army pursued the Israelites. The Book of Exodus, chapter 14, tells the story of how God enabled the Israelites to escape across the Red Sea. This is what happened:

The Lord said to Moses, 'Lift up your walking stick and hold it out over the sea. The water will divide, and the Israelites will be able to walk through the sea on dry ground... ' Moses held out his hand over the sea... The water was divided, and the Israelites went through the sea on dry ground, with walls of water on both sides. The Egyptians pursued them... The Lord said to Moses, 'Hold out your hand over the sea, and the water will come back over the Egyptians...' So Moses held out his hand over the sea, and at daybreak the water returned to its normal level. The Egyptians tried to escape from the water, but the Lord threw them into the sea.

FOR MEMORISATION

Trust in the Lord and do good. (Psalm 37:3)

THIS WEEK

The children explored the experience of persevering when they feel like giving up. They also explored the experience of making and keeping promises. They heard the story of how Moses answered God's call to free the Egyptians from their slavery in Egypt, and how he persevered when times got tough because he knew that God had promised to be with him, to help him along the way. God also promises to be with us always. We can trust that God will keep his promise.

Read together these verses from Psalm 37:

> **Psalm 37:4, 5, 7, 23–24, 28**
> Seek your happiness in the Lord,
>   and he will give you your heart's desire.
>
> Give yourself to the Lord;
>   trust in him, and he will help you …
>
> Be patient and wait for the Lord to act …
>
> The Lord guides us in the way we should go
>   and protects those who please him.
> If they fall, they will not stay down,
>   because the Lord will help them up.
>
> For the Lord loves what is right
>   and does not abandon his faithful people …

AT HOME

DID YOU KNOW?

Some scientists claim that the Red Sea experiences a huge amount of Blue Algae growth, which releases a unique dye into the water that causes it to turn red.

TIME TOGETHER

Chat Together
About the way Moses put his complete trust in God and his promises. Then name the people whom you feel you can trust and talk about why you trust them. Talk about whether you, too, are trustworthy, and whether you keep your promises. Chat about how you can always trust in God and how that makes you feel.

Invitation to Pray
Pray this prayer with your child:

Journey Prayer
Arise with me in the morning,
Travel with me through each day,
Welcome me on my arrival.
God, be with me all the way.
Amen.

Be Trustworthy
Take time to think about whether you are someone who can be trusted. Say thanks to God for the people whom you can trust.

Theme 5: Trusting God | Lesson 1: Trust in God

IN SCHOOL

THIS WEEK IN SCHOOL

You are invited to think about:
- How God helped the Chosen People to keep the covenant of love
- How you can live according to the Ten Commandments

KEY WORDS

Covenant: An agreement. God made various covenants with his people, which are recorded in the Bible.

Commandment: Something that a person is asked to do. God gave the Ten Commandments to Moses so that he would pass them on to the Israelites, his Chosen People, to help them live according to his covenant with them.

THEME 5: TRUSTING GOD | LESSON 2

Live by the Ten Commandments

ABOUT AGREEMENTS

All of us make agreements from time to time. Some of these agreements may relate to small, unimportant matters, while others may be much more significant.

- Do you remember the agreement that Orla and Josh made with their parents in the story 'Let's Go! It's Our Day!'? Would you say that was an important agreement? Why or why not?
- Did you ever make an important agreement with someone? What did you agree to do? Did you keep to the agreement?

God made several agreements with people down through the ages. These agreements were called covenants and we can read about them in the Bible.

- How many of the people with whom God made covenants can you name?

ACTIVITY

- Check the newspaper headlines to discover if there are important agreements being made now in our country or elsewhere. Share what you find with the class.

Orla and Josh

40 Grow in Love | Fourth Class/Primary 6

IN SCHOOL

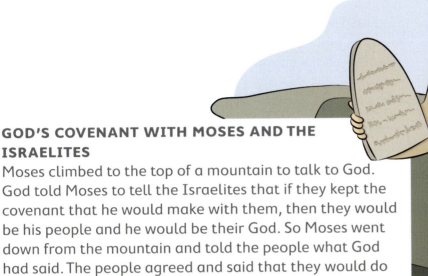

GOD'S COVENANT WITH MOSES AND THE ISRAELITES

Moses climbed to the top of a mountain to talk to God. God told Moses to tell the Israelites that if they kept the covenant that he would make with them, then they would be his people and he would be their God. So Moses went down from the mountain and told the people what God had said. The people agreed and said that they would do everything that God asked them to do. Later, God spoke to Moses again and gave him the Ten Commandments.

The Ten Commandments (Exodus 20:1-17)

God spoke, and these were his words: 'I am the Lord your God who brought you out of Egypt, where you were slaves.
Worship no God but me …
Do not use my name for evil purposes …
Observe the Sabbath and keep it holy …
Respect your father and your mother …
Do not commit murder.
Do not commit adultery.
Do not steal.
Do not accuse anyone falsely.
Do not desire another man's house; do not desire his wife, his slaves, his cattle, his donkeys, or anything else that he owns.'

FOR MEMORISATION

My trust is in you, O Lord;
 you are my God.
I am always in your care.
(Psalm 31)

ACTIVITY

- In pairs, talk about ways in which you can honour God at home, in school, in your club or in your neighbourhood. Then record some of these ways in your Religious Education journal.

DISCUSS

Talk about what your school environment is like when
- you respect one another in the classroom and in the yard
- you respect one another's property
- you are just and fair in your relationships
- you tell the truth.

Theme 5: Trusting God | Lesson 2: Live by the Ten Commandments

AT HOME

DID YOU KNOW?

When God made the covenant with Moses and the people, he promised them he would be their God and they would be his people. The people believed in God's promise.

TIME TOGETHER

Chat Together
Choose any two of the seven commandments listed on this page and talk about the ways in which they apply to your everyday lives. For instance, identify actions or words that live up to and put into practice the commandments that you have chosen; and actions or words that break or offend against those commandments.

Invitation to Pray
Good and gracious God, we thank you for the Ten Commandments. Help us to live by those commandments so that we will make the world a better place for everyone. We ask this through Jesus Christ our Lord. Amen.

Be Considerate
Life isn't easy for everyone every day. One day may be good for one person and it may be difficult for another. Think about how you might help someone who isn't having a good day.

THIS WEEK

The children heard about the covenant that God made with Moses and his people. God spoke to Moses on a mountain top and gave him the Ten Commandments. God told Moses to go and tell the leaders of the people what he had heard. The people agreed to do all that God commanded because they trusted him.

Read these seven of the Ten Commandments together:

1. I am the Lord your God, you shall not have strange gods before me.
2. You shall not take the name of the Lord your God in vain.
3. Keep the Lord's Day holy.
4. Honour your father and your mother.
5. You shall not kill.
7. You shall not steal.
8. You shall not bear false witness against your neighbour.

Grow in Love | Fourth Class/Primary 6

THEME 5: TRUSTING GOD | LESSON 3

Take Care of the Web of Life

ABOUT THE CARE OF OUR COMMON HOME

Long before you were born, generations of living beings inhabited planet Earth. When you and all the other people and animals who are alive today die, many more living creatures will continue to inhabit our planet. That is why we need to take care of it.

Pope Francis has called the earth our common home. The earth does not belong to human beings alone. We share our common home with all living species. All living things and all species are connected in a great web of life. God asks us to take care of this web of life and be good stewards of all that he has created. One way in which we can do this is by taking part in the Green/Eco-Schools programme.

IN SCHOOL

THIS WEEK IN SCHOOL

You are invited to think about:

- The web of life and how all living things are connected and dependent on one another
- Being a good steward of God's creation by living the Tenth Commandment
- The link between living by the Tenth Commandment and participating in the Green/Eco-Schools programme
- Giving thanks to God for the gift of creation

KEY WORDS

To covet: To want for yourself what belongs to another.

Interdependent: Dependent on one another. Needing one another. Sometimes the term 'interrelated' is used to describe the same thing.

Web of life: Term used to describe the interdependent relationships that exist between all living things and the earth on which we live and depend for our survival.

Steward: Someone who takes care of something without owning it.

Theme 5: Trusting God | Lesson 3: Take Care of the Web of Life

IN SCHOOL

FOR MEMORISATION

Tenth Commandment:
You shall not covet your neighbour's goods.

The Tenth Commandment asks us to be good stewards of God's creation.

ACTIVITY

Take a few moments to think about how you care for the earth and all creation. Then record in your Religious Education journal some of the things you will do to:
- conserve water at home and in school
- conserve energy at home and in school
- reduce the amount of products you use at home and in school
- recycle goods that can be recycled
- reuse some products at home or in school.

About Endangered Species

Some species in our common home are in danger of becoming extinct. This can happen for a variety of reasons. Human beings sometimes destroy the natural habitats of living things by cutting down trees to build roads and other developments. Pollution and contamination of water can be caused by careless disposal of waste from homes, factories, farms, oil refineries and many other sources. Sometimes people hunt and kill animals for their meat, fur and other valuable parts of their bodies.

ACTIVITY

- In your Religious Education journal record three endangered species and why they are endangered.

THIS WEEK
The children explored how all living things on the earth are part of the web of life, where everything is interconnected and interdependent. God invites us to take care of all the wonders he has created. When we do so, we are being good stewards of creation and we are living by the Tenth Commandment. One way we can do this is by participating in the Green/Eco-Schools programme.

Read the poem 'Trees' together.

Trees

I think that I shall never see
A poem lovely as a tree.

A tree whose hungry mouth is prest
Against the earth's sweet flowing breast;

A tree that looks at God all day,
And lifts her leafy arms to pray;

A tree that may in Summer wear
A nest of robins in her hair;

Upon whose bosom snow has lain;
Who intimately lives with rain.

Poems are made by fools like me,
But only God can make a tree.

AT HOME

DID YOU KNOW?
The Tenth Commandment teaches us to take care of the goods and property of others, and that includes caring for the planet that all living beings share. Climate change, caused mainly by the actions of human beings, is one of the greatest threats to life on earth.

TIME TOGETHER

Chat Together
About the ways you take care of the environment at home by reducing what you use, reusing and recycling waste products and so on. Chat about the ways you conserve water and energy and why it is necessary to do this. Imagine how you would like the world to be one thousand years from now.

Invitation to Pray
God, our Creator, you have given us the earth and the sky and the seas.
Show us how to care for the earth, not just for today but for ages to come.
Let no plan or work of ours damage or destroy the beauty of your creation.
Send forth your Spirit to direct us to care for the earth and all creation. Amen.

Be a Good Steward
Every small thing *you* do to care for the earth and all God's creatures counts. Every small thing *you* do makes a difference.

Theme 5: Trusting God | Lesson 3: Take Care of the Web of Life

IN SCHOOL

THIS WEEK IN SCHOOL

You are invited to think about:
- Using your gifts and talents for your own growth and for the wellbeing of others
- God's call to love everyone regardless of their religious, social or ethnic background
- The Golden Rule
- Situations where people are discriminated against

KEY WORDS

Discrimination: Unfair treatment of a particular person or group of people because of their colour, gender, religion, nationality, ethnicity, race or other personal traits.

Dignity: The respect that each one of us deserves because each one of us is a child of God and is therefore special.

THEME 5: TRUSTING GOD | LESSON 4

Living the Commandment of Love

ABOUT BEING FAIR

Recall the story 'It's Not Fair' and how Anton came home from school thinking that life was very unfair. Have you ever felt that life was unfair? If so, what made you think that?

Very often, when something seems to be unfair, it is because someone is being treated badly. Another way to describe being fair is being just and treating others properly. Do you treat others at home and at school in a fair way? How does it feel when someone doesn't treat you fairly?

ACTIVITY

- In your Religious Education journal write some slogans that encourage people to be fair.

ABOUT OUR ABILITIES

All of us have different talents and abilities. Chat about the many different talents and abilities of the people in your class. Where do these talents and abilities come from? Is it good that everyone has different talents and different abilities? Why or why not?

Why might God have given each one of us different talents and abilities? What were some of the gifts and abilities of those who took part in the Olympic Games and the Paralympics?

It's Not Fair

Grow in Love | Fourth Class/Primary 6

IN SCHOOL

Jesus always taught his disciples to love one another. Jesus never discriminated against or excluded anyone, no matter who they were or what they had done. Recall Jesus' teaching on loving God and loving your neighbour as yourself.

Here are some of the key things Jesus taught about how people should treat one another:

FOR MEMORISATION

The Golden Rule
'Do for others what you want them to do for you.'
(Luke 6:31)

The New Commandment
'Love one another. As I have loved you, so you must love one another.' (John 13:34)

The Great Commandment
'Love the Lord your God with all your heart, with all your soul, with all your strength, and with all your mind' and 'Love your neighbour as you love yourself.' (Luke 10:27)

The Golden Rule
'Do for others what you want them to do for you.' (Luke 6:31)

ACTIVITY
- Imagine Jesus is speaking the Golden Rule to you right now. In your Religious Education journal record some of the things you would like others to do for you.
- Are you prepared to do the same for them? Record some of the things you will do for others.

Theme 5: Trusting God | Lesson 4: Living the Commandment of Love

AT HOME

DID YOU KNOW?

The Golden Rule teaches us that we must treat others as we would want them to treat us.

TIME TOGETHER

Chat Together
About being fair to others in your family, in school or in your club. Is there a person at home or at school who might easily be excluded? Why might that be? What do you think Jesus asks you to do? How might you do that?
Chat about how the Golden Rule is lived in your home.

Invitation to Pray
Gracious God, you wrap us in your love each day. You sent us Jesus to show us how to love you, ourselves and our neighbour every day. You also invite us to love all living beings and the wonders of your creation. Help us by your grace and by the power of the Holy Spirit to trust you and to love you always. We ask this through Christ our Lord. Amen.

Be Inclusive
Always be careful not to exclude anyone.

THIS WEEK
The children have been exploring the different talents and abilities that God has given to each one of them. Some people may be more able than others to do certain things. A person's lack of ability in any area should never be a reason for discrimination or unfair treatment. Jesus showed us how to use our gifts and talents to love everyone and to treat everyone with dignity and respect.

Read these lines from Psalm 104 together:

> **In Praise of the Creator (Psalm 104:1, 5, 10-12)**
>
> Praise the Lord, my soul!
> O Lord, my God, how great you are! …
>
> You have set the earth firmly on its foundations,
> 　　and it will never be moved…
>
> You make springs flow in the valleys,
> 　　and rivers run between the hills.
> They provide water for the wild animals;
> 　　there the wild donkeys quench their thirst.
> In the trees near by,
> 　　the birds make their nests and sing.

Grow in Love | Fourth Class/Primary 6

THEME 6: BUILDING GOD'S KINGDOM | LESSON 1

I Have a Conscience. I Can Choose

ABOUT MAKING CHOICES

If you think about your life you will discover that you make hundreds of choices every day. Some of these choices are about small, insignificant matters, while others are about things that are very important. Some of the most important choices we make are those that involve choosing between what is right and what is wrong.
- Can you think of some choices you made today? Of choices you make on a weekly basis?
- Is it good to be free to choose? Why or why not?
- What kind of choices do you find hardest to make, and why?

ACTIVITY
- Our choices often affect other people. In your Religious Education journal record three choices you made that affected other people. They can be either good or bad choices or a mixture of good and bad.
- Talk to the person sitting next to you about those choices and how you feel about them now.

ABOUT CONSCIENCE

Our conscience helps us to judge whether something is right or wrong, and which choices we ought to make in different situations.
- Imagine you are in the schoolyard and someone falls. You can see they are hurt. What would be the right thing to do? What might you do?
- Imagine you want to buy something and you have no money. You see your gran's purse and you know there are lots of coins in it. What might you be tempted to do?
- Chat about how the choices you make can affect others.

IN SCHOOL

THIS WEEK IN SCHOOL

You are invited to think about:
- The choices you make and how these choices affect others
- How the Word of God can help you to inform your conscience
- Asking the Holy Spirit to guide the choices you make

KEY WORDS

Conscience: Conscience is the sense we have that something is right or wrong. God gives us the gift of our conscience to help us to make good judgements.

Grace: The help God gives us to live our lives in the way Jesus showed us.

Lectio Divina: A Latin phrase that means 'Sacred Reading'. *Lectio divina* is an ancient method of reading and praying with Sacred Scripture, dating back to the fourth century.

Theme 6: Building God's Kingdom | Lesson 1: I Have a Conscience. I Can Choose

IN SCHOOL

FOR MEMORISATION

Prayer to the Holy Spirit
Holy Spirit, I want to do what is right. Help me.
Holy Spirit, I want to live like Jesus. Guide me.
Holy Spirit, I want to pray like Jesus. Teach me.

God sent Jesus to show us how to make choices that are good for ourselves and for others. We can read about all that Jesus taught in the New Testament. Our parents, teachers and priests help us to understand how to do what Jesus has asked. God has given us the gift of choice. God also gives us the grace to make good choices; in other words, he helps and guides us as we make our choices. We can pray to the Holy Spirit for this grace.
- In pairs, talk about the kind of choices that are made or not made in favour of those who are most in need in our society.
- What choices can we make in relation to those people?

ABOUT GOD'S WORD AND MAKING CHOICES

When we pray and reflect on God's Word in the Bible we are guided to make good choices. The Ten Commandments helped the Chosen People in the time of Moses to live out the covenant that God had made with them. These Ten Commandments still guide us today to live as God desires.

THIS WEEK
The children have reflected on the choices they make every day and how these choices affect their lives and the lives of other people. We are gifted with a conscience to guide us in making choices.

Read the poem 'Choice' together.

Choice

A rose doesn't wake
In the morning and say,
'I think I'll wear blue
Like the bluebell today.'

Or the thrush doesn't whistle,
'I'd rather not fly
So I'll swim like the swan
And glide gracefully by.'

Or the sheep who is chewing
The grass doesn't moan,
'I wish I could chew
Like the dog on a bone.'

I can choose what to do,
I think choosing is fun.
What to wear, what to eat,
When to walk, when to run.
I can choose to be friendly
With you and with you,
And you are a person
So you can choose too.
God gave us a choice,
We are specially blessed.
So thank you and help us
To choose what is best.

AT HOME

DID YOU KNOW?
The choices we make affect ourselves, other people and the environment. They also affect our relationship with God.

TIME TOGETHER

Chat Together
About choices that you make as a family. Do you make choices together or does one person make all the choices? Chat about what can happen when some people in the family don't agree with choices that are made. What could help in such a situation?

Invitation to Pray
Prayer to the Holy Spirit
Come, Holy Spirit, fill the
    hearts of your faithful.
Enkindle in us the fire of your
    love.
Send forth your Spirit and we
    shall be created,
And you shall renew the face
    of the earth.

Be Aware
Be aware of the choices you make each day. Try to make good choices. Take time to say thanks to those who make choices that help you.

Theme 6: Building God's Kingdom | Lesson 1: I Have a Conscience. I Can Choose

IN SCHOOL

THIS WEEK IN SCHOOL

You are invited to think about:
- What the Kingdom of God is and where it is found
- What you must do to belong to the Kingdom of God

KEY WORDS

Yeast: An ingredient used in baking to make the dough rise.

A bushel: An old word for a 'bowl'.

Justice: Fairness.

THEME 6: BUILDING GOD'S KINGDOM | LESSON 2

God's Kingdom Grows Through Our Love

ABOUT LOVE AND HOW IT GROWS

We experience love in many ways. We feel loved by our family, our friends and other people. We feel loved by our pets. We, too, can love others. Sometimes it is easy to love and sometimes it is not so easy. The more we love and the more we are loved by others, the more that love grows.

God was the first to love us. God showed his love for us by giving us the gift of life and the wonders of creation. He showed us his love in a special way by sending his Son, Jesus, to live among us.
- How and where do you experience the love of God?
- How do you play your part in sharing God's love with others?

ACTIVITY

- When we love one another and do acts of love, love is spread around and it grows. In this way, the Kingdom of God grows too.
- In your Religious Education journal draw a comic strip showing ways in which you experience the different acts of love that people do each day.

ABOUT THE KINGDOM OF GOD

The Kingdom of God is also called the Reign of God. Another name by which it is known is the kingdom of heaven. Jesus taught people about the Kingdom of God through stories called parables. You have already heard the parables of the Mustard Seed, the Good Samaritan, the Lost Coin and the Widow and the Judge. All of those parables taught us something about what the Kingdom of God is like. We will now listen to some more of Jesus' parables about God's kingdom.

> **The Parable of the Yeast (Matthew 13:33)**
> Jesus told them still another parable: 'The Kingdom of heaven is like this. A woman takes some yeast and mixes it with a bushel of flour, until the whole batch of dough rises.'

52   Grow in Love | Fourth Class/Primary 6

IN SCHOOL

The Parable of the Hidden Treasure (Matthew 13:44)

'The Kingdom of heaven is like this. A man happens to find a treasure hidden in a field. He covers it up again and is so happy that he goes and sells everything he has, and then goes back and buys that field.'

The Parable of the Pearl (Matthew 13:45–46)

'Also, the Kingdom of heaven is like this. A man is looking for fine pearls, and when he finds one that is unusually fine, he goes and sells everything he has, and buys that pearl.'

DISCUSS
- What wisdom about the Kingdom of God have you found in these parables?
- Can you think of other things that the Kingdom of God could be compared to? Share your examples.

ACTIVITY
- In your Religious Education journal draw some images of how God's kingdom can be a reality in one's school, neighbourhood or in the wider world. Title your work 'The Kingdom of God'.

FOR MEMORISATION

We can help the Kingdom of God to grow by acting justly, living peacefully, loving others and caring for all of God's creation.

Theme 6: Building God's Kingdom | Lesson 2: God's Kingdom Grows Through Our Love

AT HOME

DID YOU KNOW?

In his parables Jesus always used things that the people were familiar with, such as yeast, to help them to understand his message.

TIME TOGETHER

Read
Read together the parables on pages 52 and 53.

Chat Together
About what those three parables teach you about the Kingdom of God.

Invitation to Pray
Gracious God, help us to see your kingdom rise like yeast in our world today. Help us to cherish it like the man who found the hidden treasure or the precious pearl. May we bring the justice, peace and joy of your kingdom into people's lives. Our Father in heaven, may your kingdom come. Amen.

Be Imaginative
Imagine ways you can be a builder of God's kingdom in your daily life.

THIS WEEK
In theme 3 of this programme the children were introduced to the concept of the Kingdom of God through listening to and reflecting on a number of parables. In this lesson the children explored some more of Jesus' parables, in which he compared the Kingdom of God to yeast causing dough to rise, to treasure hidden in a field and to a precious pearl. The children learned that God's kingdom exists where justice, peace, mercy and love are lived and experienced, and that God's kingdom grows and flourishes when people live by these values.

Read the poem 'Lovely Things' together.

> **Lovely Things**
>
> Bread is a lovely thing to eat –
> God bless the barley and the wheat!
>
> A lovely thing to breathe is air –
> God bless the sunshine everywhere!
>
> The earth's a lovely place to know –
> God bless the folks that come and go!
>
> Alive's a lovely thing to be –
> Giver of life – we say – bless Thee!

Grow in Love | Fourth Class/Primary 6

THEME 7: HOLY WEEK AND EASTER | LESSON 1

'Do This in Memory of Me'

ABOUT REMEMBERING
We like to remember many experiences in our lives. Can you recall stories your read? Songs you heard? Movies you saw? How different would our lives be if we didn't remember things?

ABOUT MEALS
We eat many meals alone and with others. Do you think that times when we share meals together are important occasions? Why or why not? What is the most important meal you remember? Why is it special?

ACTIVITY
- In your Religious Education journal record a menu for a meal you might like to share with your family.

ABOUT THE PASSOVER MEAL
God gave Moses the mission to free the Israelites from their slavery in Egypt and lead them to the Promised Land. Moses did as God asked. The night before their escape, the people shared a meal together. This meal has become known as the Passover meal. It is still celebrated by Jewish people today as a way of remembering how God freed them from slavery.

Moses gave instructions to the people about how the meal should be prepared and about what they should do on that night. This is what happened:

> **The First Passover (Exodus 12:21-25)**
> Moses called for all the leaders of Israel and said to them, 'Each of you is to choose a lamb or a young goat and kill it, so that your families can celebrate Passover. Take a sprig of hyssop, dip it in the bowl containing the animal's blood, and wipe the blood on the doorposts and the beam above the door of your house. Not one of you is to leave the house until morning. When the Lord goes through Egypt to kill the Egyptians, he will see the blood on the beams and on the doorposts and will not let the Angel of Death enter your houses and kill you. You and your children must obey these rules forever. When you enter the land that the Lord has promised to give you, you must perform this ritual.'

IN SCHOOL

THIS WEEK IN SCHOOL
You are invited to think about:
- Remembering and celebrating events in the life of Jesus
- The Liturgical Year

KEY WORDS
Passover: A Jewish feast that is celebrated annually to recall how God freed the Israelites from their slavery in Egypt. The word refers to how the Angel of Death 'passed over' the houses of the Israelites so that their lives would be spared.

Ritual: A ceremony or actions carried out according to specific rules or instructions.

Sprig of hyssop: A small piece of a plant of the mint family.

IN SCHOOL

ABOUT THE LAST SUPPER

Jesus invited his friends to share a Passover meal with him on the night before he died. Christians call this meal the Last Supper. At the Last Supper Jesus washed his disciples' feet. He then gave his disciples the gift of himself in bread and wine. He also gave them the New Commandment to love one another. Each time we go to Mass we remember what Jesus did and said at the Last Supper.

The Lord's Supper (Luke 22:14-20)

When the hour came, Jesus took his place at the table with the apostles. He said to them, 'I have wanted so much to eat this Passover meal with you before I suffer! ...'

Then Jesus took a cup, gave thanks to God, and said, 'Take this and share it among yourselves...'

Then [Jesus] took a piece of bread, gave thanks to God, broke it, and gave it to them, saying, 'This is my body, which is given for you. Do this in memory of me.' In the same way, he gave them the cup after the supper, saying, 'This cup is God's new covenant sealed with my blood, which is poured out for you.'

FOR MEMORISATION

'I am the bread of life.' (John 6:35)

When we celebrate the Eucharist we do as Jesus asked when he said at the Last Supper, 'Do this in memory of me.'

ACTIVITY

- In your Religious Education Journal record the words and actions of Jesus at the Last Supper in a comic strip, using speech bubbles for the words that Jesus spoke.

THIS WEEK

The children have explored the origins of the Passover meal and the story of the Last Supper. They understand that each time we celebrate the Eucharist at Mass we are doing what Jesus asked us to do when he said at the Last Supper, 'Do this in memory of me.' During our celebration of the Eucharist we remember and re-enact the words and actions of Jesus at that last meal with his disciples before he died.

Read the poem 'Remember' together.

Remember

'Remember,' Jesus said,
'Remember times we had,
Times when we were happy,
Times when we were sad,
Times we spent together
In the dark and light.
Remember our togetherness,
Remember it tonight.'

'Remember,' Jesus said,
'Remember how we shared.
When anyone had any need
Remember how we cared.
Remember how our friendship
Made every burden light.
Remember all our sharing,
Remember it tonight.'

'Remember,' Jesus said,
'Remember what I do.
I take this simple bread and wine
And give myself to you.
Remember in the days to come,
Remember when you share
This bread and wine
As friends of mine,
Remember I am there.'

AT HOME

DID YOU KNOW?

God asked the Israelites to sacrifice a lamb for the Passover meal. Jesus sacrificed his life to save us. That is why Jesus is called the Lamb of God.

TIME TOGETHER

Chat Together
About sharing meals at home and in other places. You may like to look at photos of some special meals that your family shared on particular occasions.

Invitation to Pray
Grace Before Meals
Bless us, O God, as we sit
    together.
Bless the food we eat today.
Bless the hands that made the
    food.
Bless us, O God. Amen.

Grace After Meals
Thank you, God, for the food
    we have eaten.
Thank you, God, for all our
    friends.
Thank you, God, for
    everything.
Thank you, God. Amen.

Be Mindful
Be mindful of those who make sacrifices for you. Be mindful, too, that sometimes you may need to make sacrifices for others.

Theme 7: Holy Week and Easter | Lesson 1: 'Do This in Memory of Me'

IN SCHOOL

THIS WEEK IN SCHOOL

You are invited to think about:
- Jesus' journey to Calvary
- The death of Jesus on the Cross
- The Stations of the Cross

KEY WORD

Calvary: Name of the hill on which Jesus was crucified. Also known as Golgotha.

THEME 7: HOLY WEEK AND EASTER | LESSON 2

Good Friday: Jesus Dies on the Cross

ABOUT REMEMBERING AND CELEBRATING

Each year we remember and celebrate events in our lives. Can you recall what events you mark and celebrate in your family each year? Why do you remember and celebrate those events? Do you think remembering is important? Why or why not?

ACTIVITY
- In pairs, recall the events that are remembered and celebrated in your school each year.
- In your Religious Education journal record those events, beginning with September, the start of the school year.

ABOUT HOLY WEEK

Holy Week is a very special week for Christians. During Holy Week we remember the last week in the life of Jesus. Can you recall when Holy Week begins? What are the significant events in Holy Week?

ACTIVITY
- In pairs, chat about what happens in the church during Holy Week.

IN SCHOOL

ABOUT THE STATIONS OF THE CROSS

The story of Jesus' final journey from Caiaphas' house to Calvary is recorded in art form in the fourteen Stations of the Cross. That journey is known as the Way of the Cross. We can see the Stations of the Cross in every parish church. We remember the journey that Jesus made and the people he met along the way by looking at each Station in turn while saying some prayers. We do this especially on Good Friday, the day Jesus was crucified.

ACTIVITY

- Look at the Stations of the Cross in your local church or on the internet. Can you name any of the people whom Jesus met on his journey to Calvary?

ABOUT THE TWELFTH STATION

The Twelfth Station of the Cross reminds us of Jesus' death on the Cross. We see Jesus with his arms outstretched in total surrender to his Father. Jesus is not alone. There are two thieves who have also been crucified on either side of him. One thief asks Jesus to remember him when he goes to his kingdom. Jesus promises this man that he will be with him in Paradise. Mary and John are at the foot of the Cross and they are looking at Jesus.

LOOK AND RESPOND

- Take a good look at the Twelfth Station of the Cross on this page.
- Why do you think the word 'Remember' is written on the image?
- What might the artist want us to remember when we look at this image?
- What book might it be that John is holding in his hand?

FOR MEMORISATION

'Jesus remember me when you come into your kingdom.'
(Luke 23:42)

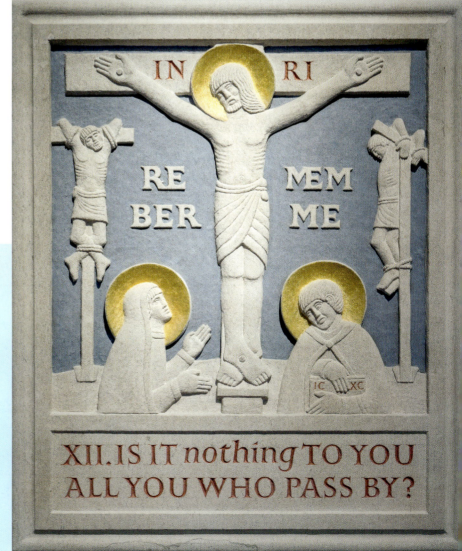

Twelfth Station of the Cross at St Mel's Cathedral, Longford by Ken Thompson

Theme 7: Holy Week and Easter | Lesson 2: Good Friday: Jesus Dies on the Cross

AT HOME

DID YOU KNOW?

There are Stations of the Cross in every Catholic church. We can use them to help us remember what happened to Jesus during his final day on earth.

TIME TOGETHER

Chat Together
About Good Friday and why it is such an important day to remember in the life of Jesus. Think about what you might do together on Good Friday. Do you think 'Good Friday' is a good name for this day? Why or why not?

Invitation to Pray
Loving Jesus, we remember the sacrifice you made for each one of us by dying on the Cross. We remember all those who are suffering today. Send your Holy Spirit to help us to reach out to someone who is suffering. Amen.

Be Attentive
Next time you visit the church you might notice the Stations of the Cross.

THIS WEEK
The children explored the Way of the Cross, the journey that Jesus made to Calvary, the place of his crucifixion and death. They learned that the milestones on that journey are recorded in the Stations of the Cross. They were introduced to the set of Stations of the Cross in St Mel's Cathedral in Longford. The children prayed the Stations of the Cross and reflected on how Jesus suffered as he walked his final journey. They discovered that Jesus was accompanied by many people along the route to Calvary.

Read the poem 'Stabat Mater' together.

Stabat Mater

At the Cross her station keeping
Stood the blessed mother weeping,
Close to Jesus to the end.

Hour of darkness descending,
Mother, Son, love unending
On the hill of Calvary.

Mary, Mary crying.
Slowly Jesus dying.
Crucified, crucified.

Head bowed, body broken,
Breath breathed, last word spoken,
'Abba, Father! Amen.'

Pieta by Michelangelo (1488-9)

IN SCHOOL

THEME 7: HOLY WEEK AND EASTER | LESSON 3

Easter: The Resurrection of Jesus

ABOUT BELIEVING

Some things are easier to believe than others. What story have you read or heard recently that you believe or don't believe? What movie have you seen where you believed that something was true or not true? List four things that you believe about yourself.

It was Mary Magdalene who first arrived at the tomb where the body of Jesus had been laid and discovered that it was empty. She ran to tell Peter and John. Then Peter and another disciple went to the tomb to see it for themselves.

THIS WEEK IN SCHOOL

You are invited to think about:
- The Resurrection of Jesus on Easter Sunday
- The shock and the delight of those who encountered Jesus on Easter Sunday morning
- The gift of peace that Jesus brings

KEY WORDS

The Resurrection: On Easter Sunday morning, three days after Jesus had been crucified, God raised Jesus to new life in a glorious body. This event is known as the Resurrection.

Alleluia: A Hebrew word that means 'God be praised'.

Rabbi: A Jewish religious leader.

Peter and John at the Tomb (John 20:3-9)

Then Peter and the other disciple went to the tomb. The two of them were running, but the other disciple ran faster than Peter and reached the tomb first. He bent over and saw the linen cloths, but he did not go in. Behind him came Simon Peter, and he went straight into the tomb. He saw the linen cloths lying there and the cloth which had been around Jesus' head. It was not lying with the linen cloths but was rolled up by itself. Then the other disciple, who had reached the tomb first, also went in; he saw and he believed. (They still did not understand the scripture which said that he must rise from death.) Then the disciples went back home.

Theme 7: Holy Week and Easter | Lesson 3: Easter: The Resurrection of Jesus

IN SCHOOL

ACTIVITIES
- In pairs, talk about how Mary Magdalene must have felt when she discovered that Jesus' body was missing from the tomb. Why do you think she ran to tell Peter and John what she had found? Do you think they would have believed Mary when she told them the story? Why or why not? Do you think you would have believed it if you had been with them? Why is that?
- Imagine one of you is Peter and the other is John and you have just arrived at the tomb and found it empty. Have a conversation about what you think might have happened to Jesus' body and about how that makes you feel.

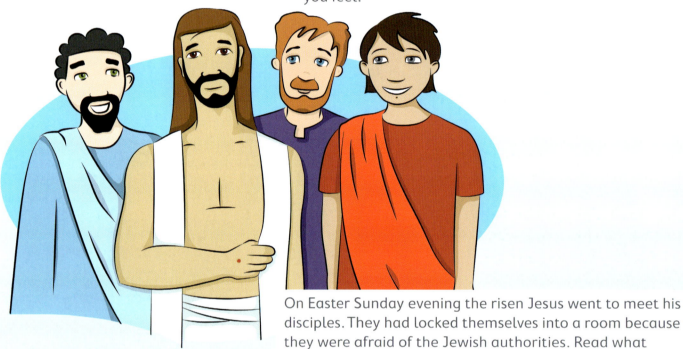

On Easter Sunday evening the risen Jesus went to meet his disciples. They had locked themselves into a room because they were afraid of the Jewish authorities. Read what happened when Jesus suddenly came and stood among them.

Jesus Appears to His Disciples (John 20:19-23)
It was late that Sunday evening, and the disciples were gathered together behind locked doors, because they were afraid of the Jewish authorities. Then Jesus came and stood among them. 'Peace be with you,' he said. After saying this, he showed them his hands and his side. The disciples were filled with joy at seeing the Lord. Jesus said to them again, 'Peace be with you. As the Father sent me, so I send you.' Then he breathed on them and said, 'Receive the Holy Spirit. If you forgive people's sins, they are forgiven; if you do not forgive them, they are not forgiven.'

FOR MEMORISATION

Prayer of St. Francis
Lord, make me an instrument of your peace:
where there is hatred, let me sow love;
where there is injury, pardon;
where there is doubt, faith;
where there is despair, hope;
where there is darkness, light;
where there is sadness, joy.

ACTIVITY
- In your Religious Education journal draw a picture of yourself offering a sign of peace to another person.

62   Grow in Love | Fourth Class/Primary 6

THIS WEEK

The children have heard the story of how Mary Magdalene was the first person to discover the empty tomb of Jesus and of how she ran to tell this news to Peter and John. They have read the Bible story of what those two disciples found when they went to the tomb to see it for themselves. They have also heard the story of how, later that evening, Jesus met a group of his disciples who had locked themselves into a room because they were afraid. Jesus offered them the gift of peace and forgiveness. The disciples were full of joy to have their Lord with them once again. The risen Jesus wants us to experience that same joy because he is with us always. We celebrate this at Easter.

Read the poem 'The Risen Jesus' together.

The Risen Jesus

He bent down, touched, reached out, healed,
He called people by their name.
He took Simon Peter's mother-in-law's hand
And helped her back on her feet again.

He was Rabbi who understood
That the hungry must be fed,
With words and deeds united as one,
In the blessing and breaking of bread.

He is the Easter story,
It is he who is raised from the dead.
He is the Easter light that shines.
He lives in the blessing and breaking of bread.

AT HOME

DID YOU KNOW?

The Church's season of Easter begins on Easter Sunday and ends on Pentecost Sunday.

TIME TOGETHER

Chat Together
About Easter time and how you will celebrate Easter. Look at the world of nature all around you for the signs of new life. Chat about times when you forgive one another at home and about all the peaceful times that you enjoy together.

Invitation to Pray
Lamb of God, you take away
    the sins of the world,
    have mercy on us.
Lamb of God, you take away
    the sins of the world,
    have mercy on us.
Lamb of God, you take away
    the sins of the world,
    grant us peace.

Be a Peacemaker
Think about times at home and at school when you could be a peacemaker. Do you know any peacemakers? Thank God for the gift of peace.

Easter garden – St. Malachy's Church, Reaghstown, Ardee, County Louth

Theme 7: Holy Week and Easter | Lesson 3: Easter: The Resurrection of Jesus

IN SCHOOL

THIS WEEK IN SCHOOL

You are invited to think about:
- The gift of service as a gift of the Holy Spirit
- How to use the gift of service

KEY WORDS

Enkindle: Set on fire.

Feast of Pentecost: Day when we remember and celebrate the coming of the Holy Spirit on the disciples of Jesus for the first time. This is the birthday of the Church.

Spiritual gifts: These are gifts we receive from the Holy Spirit that help us to serve God and to live in the way God wants us to live.

Missionary: One who continues the mission of Jesus by bringing the Good News of God's love to others.

THEME 8: THE CHURCH | LESSON 1

The Holy Spirit, Giver of Gifts

ABOUT BELONGING TO A COMMUNITY

You belong to several different communities – the community that is your family, your school community, your parish community, and perhaps some others.
- What do you think is the best thing about belonging to a community?
- How do you contribute to the communities to which you belong?
- Do you think it is a good idea to include new people in your community? Why or why not?

ACTIVITY
- In pairs, discuss the best things about your local parish community. Is there anything you would like to change?

ABOUT GIFTS

People like to give gifts and they also like to receive gifts. Both giving and receiving make us feel happy. God gives us many gifts that we can use for the benefit of all the communities to which we belong.
- Name some of the times when people receive gifts and give gifts.
- Are there occasions when you give a gift without expecting to receive one in return? When might this happen?
- What are some of the gifts God has given you?

The Holy Spirit gives us spiritual gifts. These are gifts that help us to serve God and to live in the way God wants us to live.

St Paul wrote to the people of Corinth, the Corinthians, to tell them about the gifts that the Holy Spirit brings. One of these gifts is the gift of service. Read what St Paul said:

> **Gifts from the Holy Spirit (1 Corinthians 12:4-7)**
> There are different kinds of spiritual gifts, but the same Spirit gives them. There are different ways of serving, but the same Lord is served. There are different abilities to perform service, but the same God gives ability to all for their particular service. The Spirit's presence is shown in some way in each person for the good of all.

IN SCHOOL

ACTIVITY
- Think about the different jobs people do, e.g. nurse, doctor, cleaner, teacher, caretaker, secretary, electrician, soldier, farmer, etc.
- Choose three of the occupations you identified. In your Religious Education journal record the variety of gifts and abilities that people bring to these jobs.

Every year the Church celebrates the feast of Pentecost. On this feast Christians remember when God sent the Holy Spirit on the disciples of Jesus for the first time, and out of that the Church was born. Read what happened:

The Coming of the Holy Spirit (Acts of the Apostles 2:1-13)

When the day of Pentecost came, all the believers were gathered together in one place. Suddenly there was a noise from the sky which sounded like a strong wind blowing, and it filled the whole house where they were sitting. Then they saw what looked like tongues of fire which spread out and touched each person there. They were all filled with the Holy Spirit and began to talk in other languages, as the Spirit enabled them to speak.

There were Jews living in Jerusalem, religious people who had come from every country in the world. When they heard this noise, a large crowd gathered. They were all excited, because all of them heard the believers talking in their own languages. In amazement and wonder they exclaimed, 'These people who are talking like this are Galileans! How is it, then, that all of us hear them speaking in our own native languages?... Some of us are from Rome, both Jews and Gentiles converted to Judaism, and some of us are from Crete and Arabia – yet all of us hear them speaking in our own languages about the great things that God has done!' Amazed and confused, they kept asking each other, 'What does this mean?'

But others made fun of the believers, saying, 'These people are drunk!'

FOR MEMORISATION

There are different kinds of spiritual gifts, but the same Spirit gives them. The Spirit's presence is shown in some way in each person for the good of all. (1 Corinthians 12:4, 7)

ACTIVITY
- Find a partner. One of you will pretend that you were present when the Holy Spirit came upon the believers on the first Pentecost in Jerusalem, and the other will pretend to be someone who lived in Jerusalem at that time but who was not present on that occasion. Act out the conversation that the two of you might have had later that day.

Theme 8: The Church | Lesson 1: The Holy Spirit, Giver of Gifts

AT HOME

DID YOU KNOW?
The feast of Pentecost is celebrated on the seventh Sunday after Easter every year.

TIME TOGETHER

Chat Together
About how, by doing acts of love for others, you can help to build a just and peaceful society.

Invitation to Pray
Prayer to the Holy Spirit
Come, Holy Spirit, fill the hearts of your faithful.
Enkindle in us the fire of your love.
Send forth your Spirit and we shall be created
And you shall renew the face of the earth.

O God, who has taught the hearts of the faithful
By the light of the Holy Spirit,
Grant us in the same Spirit to be truly wise
And ever to rejoice in his consolation,
Through Christ our Lord. Amen.

Be Joyful
As you do acts of love for one another this Easter time, be joyful that the Holy Spirit is there to guide you always.

THIS WEEK
The children heard the story of what happened at the first Pentecost, when the Holy Spirit came upon the disciples of Jesus for the first time. They also heard what St Paul wrote to the people of Corinth about the gifts of the Holy Spirit. The children explored one of these gifts, the gift of service.

Read the poem 'Pentecost: I Was There' together.

Pentecost: I Was There

I was there when Peter barred the door.
I watched the others silent in the gloom,
Each pair of eyes so sad and far away,
Each saddened heart remembering the tomb.
Then Andrew said, 'Remember on the lake,
Remember how he called my brother out';
And Peter said, 'My heart was light and free,
And half way there it sank with fear and doubt';
And now the voices rang around the room
As others told a tale from days gone by
Of lepers healed, the mad man soothed and stilled,
A new day dawning in a blind man's eye,
Of children loved, a Roman soldier's hope,
A lame man filled with joy at new-found feet.
And with their hearts brim full of joy and peace
They ran and brought that message to the street.
I was there when hearts were closed and sad,
When hearts were opened, gladdened and set free.
I sat in silence in the upper room.
Yes I was there that day, and so was he.

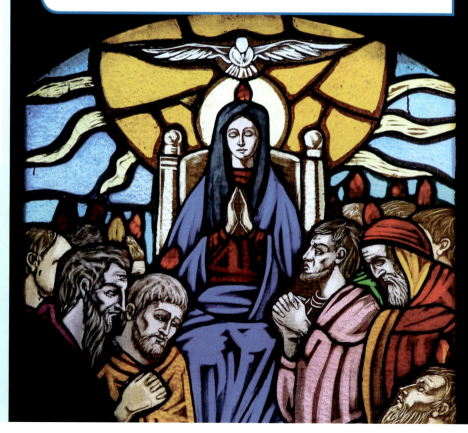

66 Grow in Love | Fourth Class/Primary 6

IN SCHOOL

THEME 8: THE CHURCH | LESSON 2

The Church is One Family of God

ABOUT TEAMWORK

People grow closer together – they build unity - when they work together as part of a team. Think of your favourite sports team and how close they seem to be as they all work together to achieve a common goal. Your class is a team, too, and so is your family and your parish community.

- Do you think it is a good thing to belong to a team? Why or why not?
- What teams do you know that work well together? Why might that be?

ACTIVITIES

- In pairs, discuss whether working as a member of a team is better than working on your own. Name some things that can only be done by a team rather than by an individual.
- Now discuss groups that you know that work for a common purpose. Then record some of these groups and the kind of work they do in your Religious Education journal.

ABOUT OUR UNITY AS CHRISTIANS

Christians are one big family – the family of God. All Christians are united in their belief that there is one God, whose Son, Jesus, lived among us and rose from the dead. While Christians may belong to different church families, all Christians also believe that God sent the Holy Spirit to be with us to guide us on our journey to our common home in heaven.

When people of different Christian Churches come together to work towards a common goal, we call it ecumenism. Many of the leaders of the different Christian Churches, for example, come together to talk about the things they have in common and to think of ways in which they can build on that unity.

THIS WEEK IN SCHOOL

You are invited to think about:
- Working as a member of a team
- How all Christians are united
- Praying for unity between the Christian Churches

KEY WORDS

Christians: Name for those who have been baptized and who believe in Jesus Christ, the Son of the one God, and in his Resurrection.

Ecumenism: A term used to describe the efforts Christians make to bring about unity among the different Christian Churches.

Repent: To be sorry for our sins and to seek God's forgiveness.

Theme 8: The Church | Lesson 2: The Church is One Family of God

IN SCHOOL

Pope Francis with Russian Orthodox Patriarch Kirill of Moscow

FOR MEMORISATION

There is one God and Father of all people. (Ephesians 4:6)

St Paul, in his letter to the Christians in the city of Ephesus, encouraged them to work together in peace. Here is one statement from that letter, in which he speaks about the unity that should unite all Christians:

The Unity of Christians (Ephesians 4:5–7)

There is one Lord, one faith, one baptism; there is one God and Father of all people, who is Lord of all, works through all, and is in all.

ACTIVITY

- In your Religious Education journal record some of the things that unite you with other Christians.

'One Lord, one faith, one baptism'

THIS WEEK
The children explored what it means to work as a member of a team and why working as part of a team is usually better than working on your own. They also explored some of the key beliefs that unite all members of the Christian family.

Read the poem 'Us' together.

> **Us**
>
> I know a little tiny word –
> It's small, but it's fantastic.
> It'll stretch to cover a multitude
> Because it's made of elastic.
>
> It stretches over families,
> It covers neighbours and friends,
> It fits all nations and peoples,
> From here to the world's very end.
>
> It stretches and stretches until –
> Oh dear! I fear it will burst!
> But it doesn't; it snaps itself back
> To its original – US!

AT HOME

DID YOU KNOW?
Every year all Christian Churches devote one week to praying for Christian unity. Christian Unity Week takes place between 18 and 25 January.

TIME TOGETHER

Chat Together
About good times you enjoy together as a family. Chat about when your family works really well together. What things do you like doing together as a family? Do you ever join in with other families to do things together? What is that like?

Invitation to Pray
Pray *The Apostles' Creed* together.

Be United
Look out for ways you can become more involved in your parish community – and by so doing become more united with the other members of your Church.

Theme 8: The Church | Lesson 2: The Church is One Family of God

IN SCHOOL

THIS WEEK IN SCHOOL

You are invited to think about:
- The Church as a people gathered together to continue the mission of Jesus
- Why the family is called a 'domestic church'
- The role of the Holy Spirit in prompting people to share the Good News

KEY WORDS

Mission: A task or job that is given to a person or group of people.

Mission of the Church: The mission of the Church is to continue the work that Jesus gave to his disciples. Above all, it is to share the Good News of God's love with all people.

Missionaries: People who continue the mission of Jesus by sharing the Good News.

THEME 8: THE CHURCH | LESSON 3

Continuing the Mission of Jesus Today

ABOUT ASSEMBLIES AND GATHERINGS

People gather in groups in many places each day for a variety of reasons. Can you think of some places where people gather and why they do so? Members of the Church gather to worship and to celebrate their faith together as one family – the family of God.

ABOUT THE MISSION OF JESUS

God gave Jesus a mission when he sent him to live on earth. This is how Jesus described his mission:

> **Jesus' Mission (Lk 4:16-20)**
> 'The Spirit of the Lord is upon me,
>   because he has chosen me to bring good news to the poor.
> He has sent me to proclaim liberty to the captives
>   and recovery of sight to the blind,
> to set free the oppressed
>   and announce that the time has come
>   when the Lord will save his people.'

ACTIVITY
- See if you can recall and share some stories from the Bible of Jesus carrying out the mission that he described in the above passage.

70   Grow in Love | Fourth Class/Primary 6

IN SCHOOL

THE CHURCH CONTINUES THE MISSION OF JESUS TODAY

Before he returned to his Father in heaven, Jesus asked his disciples to continue the work that he had begun – to bring the Good News of God's love to all people, especially to the poor and to those in most need. He promised that he would send the Holy Spirit to be with them to help them with this work. This promise was fulfilled on the day of Pentecost, when the Holy Spirit came upon the followers of Jesus.

Christians all over the world today continue to carry out the same mission that Jesus gave the first disciples. In Baptism, God sends the Holy Spirit to us to give us the courage to do this work.

ACTIVITIES
- In pairs, chat about the ways you can continue the mission of Jesus.
- In your Religious Education journal record some things you can do with your family to carry out the mission of Jesus.

FOR MEMORISATION

Prayer to the Holy Spirit
Come, Holy Spirit, fill the hearts of your faithful.
Enkindle in us the fire of your love.
Send forth your Spirit and we shall be created,
And you shall renew the face of the earth.

O God, who has taught the hearts of the faithful
By the light of the Holy Spirit,
Grant us in the same Spirit to be truly wise
And ever to rejoice in his consolation,
Through Christ our Lord.
Amen.

Theme 8: The Church | Lesson 3: Continuing the Mission of Jesus Today

AT HOME

DID YOU KNOW?

The family is called 'the domestic church'. That is because the first place where we learn about our faith, and where our faith is nurtured, is in our own home.

TIME TOGETHER

Chat Together
About the ways that you as a family can continue the mission of Jesus. What can you do to help someone in need in your family or in your local community? Everyone can't go to far-off places like Kenya to work as missionaries. Are there ways that your family can support the work of those who do?

Invitation to Pray
Holy Spirit, help us to continue Jesus' mission of bringing God's love to others whenever and wherever we can. Guide us to recognise ways in which we can do this.

Be Aware
Be aware of the opportunities that you have as a family to carry out the mission of Jesus at home and in your local community.

THIS WEEK
The children learned that the Church is a community of believers who continue the mission of Jesus by sharing the Good News of God's love for everyone. They also learned that people who share the Good News are called missionaries, and that they, too, can be missionaries – at home, in school and in their neighbourhood or parish.

Read this extract from the journal of Maura Lee, who worked as a lay missionary in Kenya:

> **Maura Lee's Story**
> My journey to Kenya began in 2009 on hearing that the Daughters of Charity of Saint Vincent de Paul had opened two centres to support people who were living in poor circumstances. … Because of their situations and their struggles with poverty, their daily focus was on getting the food and water they needed to stay alive.
>
> One morning, as I was on my way to do some home visits with the community nurse, I passed a little boy sitting at the side of the road. He told me that the teacher wouldn't let him into school, as his parents hadn't paid the school fees. Just then, the stillness of the air was filled with young, happy voices as the playground filled with children. The little boy rushed to the gates, held two bars with each of his small hands and rested his head in the gap between; he had such a longing desire to be on the other side of the gate. It wasn't his fault that his parents hadn't the money to pay the fees. They weren't working because the rains hadn't come and they couldn't earn money weeding the crops for farmers, as they usually did.

Grow in Love | Fourth Class/Primary 6

THEME 8: THE CHURCH | LESSON 4

Working for Christian Unity

ABOUT CHRISTIANS

'Christ' is one of the titles for Jesus and it is from this name that we get the word 'Christian'. Christians are followers of Jesus. Jesus wants all Christians to work together for peace and unity.

ABOUT THE CHRISTIAN FAMILY

The five Christian Churches that we will explore this week are the Catholic Church, the Church of Ireland, the Methodist Church, the Presbyterian Church and the Orthodox Church.
- Are there different Christian Churches in your locality? Can you name them?
- What do you know about any of these other members of the Christian family?

RESEARCH

- If possible, and with the permission of a parent or guardian, make contact with someone from your locality who belongs to another Christian Church and interview them using these or similar questions:
  – What prayers do you say?
  – When do you go to church and what happens there?
  – Who are the leaders in your Church?
  – Does your Church encourage its members to read the Bible? Is the Bible read aloud in your church?
- Tell the class what you learned about this other Christian Church from your interview.

IN SCHOOL

THIS WEEK IN SCHOOL

You are invited to think about:
- The five Christian Churches you have heard about – Catholic, Church of Ireland, Methodist, Presbyterian and Orthodox
- God as the Good Shepherd to all people

KEY WORD

Christ: One of the titles given to Jesus.

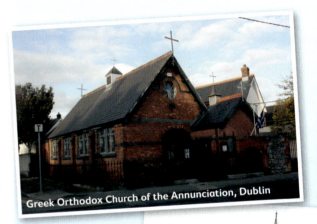
Greek Orthodox Church of the Annunciation, Dublin

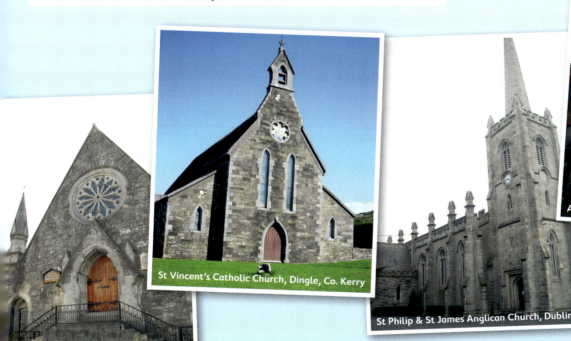
Athlone Methodist Church, Athlone
St Vincent's Catholic Church, Dingle, Co. Kerry
St Philip & St James Anglican Church, Dublin
Abbey Presbyterian Church, Dublin

Churches of different Christian denominations in Ireland

Theme 8: The Church | Lesson 4: Working for Christian Unity

IN SCHOOL

FOR MEMORISATION

Agnus Dei
Lamb of God, you take away the sins of the world,
   have mercy on us.
Lamb of God, you take away the sins of the world,
   have mercy on us.
Lamb of God, you take away the sins of the world,
   grant us peace.

CHRISTIAN UNITY WEEK

Christian Unity Week is celebrated every year from 18 to 25 January. During this week Christians from different Churches in various cultures and traditions pray for unity among all Christians. Christians are reminded that while there are many differences between the various Christian Churches, we are all united in the one family of Christ.

Jesus told his followers that people should be able to recognise Christians by the love they show towards one another.

ACTIVITIES

- In pairs, chat about what Christians around the world might pray for. In your Religious Education journal record some of the examples you identify.
- Name some projects that people from the different Christian Churches might join together to work on.

THIS WEEK

The children learned about some of the other Christian Churches that are part of the Christian community. They explored how Christians from these different Churches can create unity between one another by praying together and by working together on issues that are common to all people.

Read the poem 'Making Peace' together.

> **Making Peace**
>
> Making PEACE isn't easy!
> I start it with P
> For Patience with someone
> Who's different to me.
> Then E is for Everyone –
> How can that be?
> I've more than enough love
> Inside me, you see.
> And A is for Always,
> Not just for today,
> At home and at school
> When I run out to play.
> And C is for Caring,
> That's doing what's good,
> Not just when I have to
> Or ought to, or should.
> And E is for Ever
> As Jesus has planned.
> Oh, make PEACE in my heart, Lord,
> And PEACE in our land.

AT HOME

DID YOU KNOW?

In the Gospel according to St Matthew Jesus told Peter that we have to forgive one another not seven times but seventy times seven.

TIME TOGETHER

Chat Together
About the Church to which you belong and what it means to you.

Invitation to Pray
Loving God, we thank you for the gifts of peace and unity. We ask you for the grace to help us
- have peace in our hearts,
- build peace in our families,
- build peace in our school,
- build peace where we live,
- build peace in our country and our world.

We ask this through Christ our Lord. Amen.

Be a Peacemaker
Ask God to help you recognise the people with whom you need to make peace.

Theme 8: The Church | Lesson 4: Working for Christian Unity

IN SCHOOL

THIS WEEK IN SCHOOL

You are invited to think about:
- Why people go on pilgrimage
- Some of the activities people do when they are on pilgrimage
- The importance of World Youth Day

KEY WORDS

Jubilee: This is a Holy Year announced by the Pope.

Pilgrimage: A journey made by people of faith to a holy site.

Marian pilgrimage: A pilgrimage to a holy place devoted to the Blessed Virgin Mary.

THEME 9: THE PILGRIM CHURCH | LESSON 1

Pilgrimages at Home and Abroad

ABOUT PILGRIMAGES TO MARIAN SHRINES

People of faith have gone on pilgrimages to holy sites down through the centuries. They believe it helps them to connect with God in a special way.

In Ireland, many people go on pilgrimage to the Marian Shrine at Knock, where Our Lady once appeared to a group of local people. Some also travel with a parish group to the Marian Shrine at Lourdes in France, where Our Lady appeared to St Bernadette.

Pilgrimages to Marian shrines give people an opportunity to ask Mary, our Mother, to help them to live with faith and trust in God, as she did. Mary is always willing to listen to us and to bring our prayers to Jesus.

ACTIVITIES

- In pairs, share your thoughts on why you feel Our Lady appeared to St Bernadette in Lourdes and to a group of local people in Knock.
- In your Religious Education journal write a short letter to Mary, our Mother. Tell her something positive that you are grateful for in your life at this time. Mention also any concerns you may have about anyone or anything. You might like to finish your letter with the words 'Our Lady of Knock, pray for us' or 'Our Lady of Lourdes, pray for us'.

ABOUT PILGRIMAGES TO CROAGH PATRICK

St Patrick is believed to have spent the forty days of Lent on Croagh Patrick in County Mayo. Every year, on the last Sunday in July, thousands of pilgrims from all around the world gather at Croagh Patrick for what is called 'Reek Sunday'. Many climb the mountain barefoot. It is a day of prayer. Outdoor Masses are celebrated throughout the day and people may go to confession in St Patrick's Chapel.

- How do you think climbing Croagh Patrick might help people to feel closer to God?
- Is there a special place that you go to when you want to pray to or be alone with God?

Pilgrims climbing Croagh Patrick in County Mayo

76

Grow in Love | Fourth Class/Primary 6

IN SCHOOL

Pilgrims carrying the World Youth Day Cross

ABOUT WORLD YOUTH DAY PILGRIMAGES

The first World Youth Day (WYD) was held in Rome, Italy in 1986. Since then, every Palm Sunday has been declared a WYD. Every second or third year this is a big international event that takes place in a particular city somewhere in the world, at which the Pope delivers a special message to the millions of young pilgrims. On these occasions the young people carry the World Youth Day Cross in procession as a symbol of the love of Christ for all people. In the years when there is no international event, the celebrations take place in the local dioceses of the different countries.

FOR MEMORISATION

'As the Father sent me, so am I sending you.' (John 20:21; the theme for World Youth Day, Manila, Philippines, 1995)

ACTIVITY

- Imagine you are invited to write a letter to the Pope suggesting ideas for a World Children's Day of Faith. You may wish to find a partner to discuss and share ideas before you begin your letter. Here are some questions to get you started:
  - Why do you think it is important to have a World Children's Day of Faith?
  - What passage from Sacred Scripture might you choose as a theme for this special event?
  - What activities do you suggest should be included that would appeal to children?
  - Where and how often might this pilgrimage take place?
- Write the letter in your Religious Education journal.

Theme 9: The Pilgrim Church | Lesson 1: Pilgrimages at Home and Abroad

AT HOME

DID YOU KNOW?

Thousands of young people from Ireland travel to other parts of the world to attend World Youth Days. They usually travel with groups from their dioceses.

TIME TOGETHER

Chat Together
Have you ever gone on a pilgrimage or do you know anyone who has? Do you think going on a pilgrimage is a good thing to do? Why or why not? Take time together to look at the prayer of praise your child composed in their Religious Education journal.

Invitation to Pray
Pray these words from the *Magnificat*, the hymn of thanksgiving sung by Our Lady on the occasion of her visit to her cousin Elizabeth.

The Magnificat
My soul proclaims the greatness of the Lord,
my spirit rejoices in God my Saviour;
For he has looked with favour on his lowly servant,
and from this day all generations will call me blessed.
The Almighty has done great things for me:
holy is his name.

Be Grateful
Be grateful for all those pilgrims who pray for others when they go on pilgrimage.

THIS WEEK
The children have been learning more about pilgrimages at home and abroad. As well as recalling why people go on pilgrimage to Marian shrines such as Knock and Lourdes, they have heard the story of St Patrick spending the forty days of Lent on Croagh Patrick. This is recalled each year in the Reek Pilgrimage that is held on Croagh Patrick. The children have also learned about the World Youth Day (WYD) pilgrimage event that was started by St John Paul II.

Invite your child to tell you what they have learned about pilgrimages this week.

Map showing the location of the Marian Shrines at Knock, Lourdes and Fatima

Our Lady of Fatima

Grow in Love | Fourth Class/Primary 6

THEME 9: THE PILGRIM CHURCH | LESSON 2

Our Lady of Guadalupe

ABOUT IMAGES OF MARY

It can be lovely to look back at photographs of happy times we have spent with family and friends. Sometimes people in those photographs may no longer be with us, so we can treasure and keep their memory alive by looking at pictures of them and recalling happy times spent with them.

There were no cameras in the time when Mary, the Mother of God, lived on earth, so artists down the centuries have made representations of what they think she may have looked like. They have been helped in this task by the descriptions of Mary given by those to whom she appeared, as well as by the stories about her in the Bible.

- Look at all the images of Mary on the *Grow in Love* poster. What do you think these images tell us about Mary?
- Do you think Mary's different titles match the different images. Why or why not?

LOOK AND RESPOND

- Take some time on your own to look at the images of Mary.
- Select the image that appeals most to you. Tell the class or the child sitting next to you why you like that image.

IN SCHOOL

THIS WEEK IN SCHOOL

You are invited to think about:
- The apparition of Our Lady at Guadalupe
- Giving thanks to God for the gift of Mary, Mother of all people and Queen of heaven and earth

KEY WORDS

Apparition: An unexpected appearance.

Intercession: Request on behalf of another person.

Indigenous: Native to a particular place.

Grotto near the Basilica of Our Lady of Guadalupe, Mexico

Theme 9: The Pilgrim Church | Lesson 2: Our Lady of Guadalupe

IN SCHOOL

Here is the story of the apparition of Our Lady to Juan Diego at Guadalupe in Mexico:

> ### The Apparition of Our Lady of Guadalupe, Mexico (1531)
>
> One day in 1531, a young boy named Juan Diego from Guadalupe was walking past Tepeyac Hill on his way to Mass when he saw a beautiful woman standing on the hill. The woman was surrounded by a ball of sunlight. She spoke to Juan in his native language and said: 'My dear son, I love you. I desire you to know who I am. I am the ever-virgin Mary, Mother of the true God who gives life to all living things. He created all things. He is in all places. He is Lord of heaven and earth. I would like to have a church built in this place where your people may come to pray and experience my compassion. All those who come here can ask for my help in their work and in their sorrows. I will help them like a mother helps her children. So run now to Tenochtitlan and tell the bishop all that you have seen and heard.'

FOR MEMORISATION

Pilgrimages in honour of Mary are called Marian pilgrimages

ACTIVITY
- Imagine you met Juan Diego on his way to visit the bishop. Find a partner and act out the conversation.

At first the bishop didn't believe Juan's story, but when Juan visited him again and showed him the image of Mary on his tilma, or cloak, the bishop was convinced that the apparition really had taken place. More and more people heard the story of the appearance of Our Lady to Juan Diego and Guadalupe soon became a place of pilgrimage to Our Lady. Today, Guadalupe is the most visited Marian shrine in the world and Juan Diego is now a saint.

ACTIVITY
- In your Religious Education journal record some of the remarkable facts about the tilma containing the image of Our Lady of Guadalupe.

Statue of St Juan Diego in North Carolina, USA

THIS WEEK
The children have heard the story of the apparition of Our Lady to Juan Diego in Guadalupe, Mexico. She wanted him to know God, the Creator of all life, and to tell others about God and his love for all people. The children have also been introduced to the *Memorare*, one of the oldest and best known of all Marian prayers. When we pray to Mary our Mother in faith, we can be assured that she will bring our prayers to her Son, Jesus.

Read and pray the *Memorare* together.

The Memorare
Remember, O most gracious Virgin Mary,
that never was it known that anyone
who fled to your protection,
implored your help or sought your
intercession was left unaided.
Inspired with this confidence, I fly unto you,
O Virgin of virgins, my Mother.
To you do I come. Before you I stand,
sinful and sorrowful.
O Mother of the Word Incarnate,
despise not my petitions,
but in your mercy hear and answer me. Amen.

AT HOME

DID YOU KNOW?
By 1539, only eight years after the apparition of Our Lady to Juan Diego, an estimated eight million of the Aztec people of Mexico had converted to Catholicism.

TIME TOGETHER

Chat Together
About the different places where Our Lady appeared. See if you can remember one thing about each apparition. Which of these places would you most like to visit? Why? Share some of the interesting facts about the tilma containing the image of Our Lady of Guadalupe.

Invitation to Pray
Pray the *Hail Mary* together.

Be Curious
Find out more about another Marian pilgrimage site that you have heard about or that you find interesting.

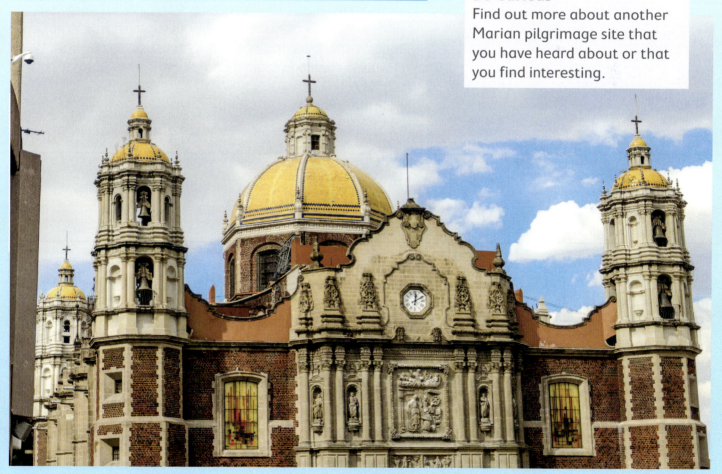

The original Basilica of Our Lady of Guadalupe, completed in 1709

Theme 9: The Pilgrim Church | Lesson 2: Our Lady of Guadalupe

IN SCHOOL

THIS WEEK IN SCHOOL

You are invited to think about:
- Times when you repented and received the gift of forgiveness
- Giving thanks to God for the gift of his unconditional love and forgiveness

KEY WORDS

Sin: Anything we do or say that breaks Jesus' law of love and weakens or destroys our friendship with God.

Mortal Sin: This is a serious sin that destroys our friendship with God.

Venial Sin: This is a less serious type of sin than mortal sin. However, repeatedly committing venial sins can also be very damaging to our relationship with God.

Unconditional love: This is love that has no conditions. God's love is unconditional. God will always love us.

THEME 10: RECONCILIATION | LESSON 1

God Forgives Us

Recall the story of Jodi and her dad. Which of Jodi's words or actions would you say were not in keeping with the way God wants us to act or with the kind of person God wants each of us to be?

ABOUT GOD'S LOVE AND FORGIVENESS

Jesus' mission was to share the Good News of God's unconditional love for all people. In other words, Jesus wanted to show people what God's love was like and to tell them that God would always love them. Jesus asks us to copy his way of living so that we, too, can be examples of God's love in action in the world today.

Sometimes we act in ways that are not in keeping with the way God wants us to act or with the kind of person God wants us to be. When we act in this way, we sin. Jesus showed us that when we fail to live as God wants us to live, we can always return to God. All we need to do is be sorry and ask for God's forgiveness. God is always ready to forgive us.

RECALL AND DISCUSS

- Recall the story 'The Forgiving Stone'. What does this story teach us about the different types of sin? What does it teach us about what we must do to obtain forgiveness, no matter whether our sins are big or small?

The Forgiving Stone

Grow in Love | Fourth Class/Primary 6

IN SCHOOL

ACTIVITY
Look at the pictures on this page, each of which illustrates a story you have heard in which Jesus showed us or told us what God's forgiveness is like.
- With a partner, identify each story.
- Then share what each story teaches us about God's forgiveness.
- Tell your partner which story you prefer, and why.

ABOUT THE SACRAMENT OF RECONCILIATION
Jesus brought God's loving mercy and forgiveness to all when he was on earth. Today, we can experience that same love, mercy and forgiveness in the Sacrament of Reconciliation. When we are truly sorry and when we ask for God's forgiveness in this sacrament, God forgives our sins through the words and actions of the priest and he welcomes us back into his love. God forgives all sins, both large (mortal) and small (venial), when we are truly sorry and repent.

FOR MEMORISATION
The Lord is merciful and good. (Psalm 116:5)

Theme 10: Reconciliation | Lesson 1: God Forgives Us

83

AT HOME

DID YOU KNOW?

In 2013, when Cardinal Bergoglio accepted his election to the papacy as Pope Francis, he said, 'I am a sinner, but I trust in the infinite mercy and patience of our Lord Jesus Christ.'

TIME TOGETHER

Chat Together
About the need for both love and forgiveness in our lives. Share your memories of times when you needed, wanted and received forgiveness from others in your family. Try to remember what we do when we celebrate the Sacrament of Reconciliation. Perhaps you can make time to visit your local church to celebrate this sacrament.

Invitation to Pray
Pray together the *Prayer for Forgiveness* which you will find with the other prayers at the back of this book.

Be Grateful
Be grateful for the times when you sought and received forgiveness from others. Be grateful, too, for God's forgiveness, which is always available to us.

THIS WEEK
The children have been learning about God's constant and unconditional love for us, and that God forgives all sins, both large (mortal) and small (venial), when we repent and ask for his forgiveness. They also learned that all sins damage our relationship with God and with other people. But just as Jesus brought God's loving mercy and forgiveness to all when he was on earth, today Jesus continues to offer us God's love, mercy and forgiveness in the Sacrament of Reconciliation. From God's constant love comes the wonderful gift of forgiveness.

Pray together these prayers which we say at Mass. The parent or guardian may read out the words of the priest and the child read out the response.

Priest: Have mercy on us, O Lord.
Response: For we have sinned against you.

Priest: Show us, O Lord, your mercy.
Response: And grant us your salvation.

Priest: May almighty God have mercy on us,
forgive us our sins,
and bring us to everlasting life.
Response: Amen.

Pope Francis receives absolution at St Peter's, Vatican City

THEME 10: RECONCILIATION | LESSON 2

God Calls Us to Forgive Others

ABOUT THE *OUR FATHER*

When Jesus' disciples asked him to teach them how to pray, he taught them the *Our Father*. The words of this prayer in the Bible are slightly different from those that we have learned, but it is the same prayer. The *Our Father* is the only formal prayer that Jesus gave us and it includes his teaching about forgiveness. In the New Testament we hear Jesus say: '… forgive us the wrongs we have done, as we forgive the wrongs that others have done to us' (Matthew 6:12). We use different words – 'forgive us our trespasses, as we forgive those who trespass against us' – to say exactly the same thing. The *Our Father* is sometimes called the *Lord's Prayer*.

ACTIVITY

- On another occasion, Peter asked Jesus how many times should we forgive those who hurt or offend us. Jesus replied, 'Not seven times, but seventy times seven' (Matthew 18:22).
- Talk to the child sitting next to you about what you think Jesus was teaching here about how we should forgive others. Was he really interested in the numbers he mentioned, or was he just using them to teach us something about forgiveness?
- Then, in your Religious Education journal, record how you think this teaching of Jesus about forgiveness applies to your life and your relationships with others.

IN SCHOOL

THIS WEEK IN SCHOOL

You are invited to think about:
- Times when you were forgiven
- Ways in which you can be a more forgiving person

KEY WORD

Trespass: Today, this word is most often used to mean 'entering someone else's property without permission'. In the *Our Father*, however, it refers to actions that are wrong or sinful. We pray: '… forgive us our trespasses, as we forgive those who trespass against us.'

Jesus teaches Peter about forgiveness

IN SCHOOL

Jesus taught us about how we are challenged to forgive others, as God forgives us, in the Parable of the Unforgiving Servant.

The Parable of the Unforgiving Servant (Matthew 18:23-35)

Jesus said, '… the Kingdom of heaven is like this. Once there was a king who decided to check on his servants' accounts. He had just begun to do so when one of them was brought in who owed millions of dollars. The servant did not have enough to pay his debt, so the king ordered him to be sold as a slave, with his wife and his children and all that he had, in order to pay the debt. The servant fell on his knees before the king. "Be patient with me," he begged, "and I will pay you everything!" The king felt sorry for him, so he forgave him the debt and let him go.

Then the man went out and met one of his fellow servants who owed him a few dollars. He grabbed him and started choking him. "Pay back what you owe me!" he said. His fellow servant fell down and begged him, "Be patient with me, and I will pay you back!" But he refused; instead, he had him thrown into jail until he should pay the debt. When the other servants saw what had happened, they were very upset and went to the king and told him everything. So he called the servant in. "You worthless slave!" he said "I forgave you the whole amount you owed me, just because you asked me to. You should have had mercy on your fellow servant, just as I had mercy on you." The king was very angry, and he sent the servant to jail to be punished until he should pay back the whole amount.'

And Jesus concluded, 'That is how my Father in heaven will treat every one of you unless you forgive your brother from your heart.'

FOR MEMORISATION

Forgive us our trespasses, as we forgive those who trespass against us.

DISCUSS
- Chat with a partner about what this parable teaches about forgiveness.

ACTIVITY
- God calls us to forgive others. In your Religious Education journal record three examples of people showing forgiveness towards those who have hurt or offended them.

86 | Grow in Love | Fourth Class/Primary 6

THIS WEEK

The children have been learning more about God's love and forgiveness. They have heard Jesus' teaching about forgiveness in the Parable of the Unforgiving Servant. God loves us and is always ready to give us the gift of forgiveness. But God wants us, too, to forgive others, just as he forgives us. Sometimes, forgiving others can be very difficult.

Pray this prayer together:

> Loving Jesus, thank you for the gift of forgiveness. Help us to forgive others when they hurt us, just as you forgive us. We ask Mary, our Mother, and all the angels and saints, to help us live in the way you showed us – loving God and loving others with all our hearts. Amen.

AT HOME

DID YOU KNOW?

At Mass we ask God for forgiveness when we pray: 'Lord, have mercy. Christ, have mercy.'

TIME TOGETHER

Chat Together

Share your memories of times when you found it easy to forgive someone and times when you found it difficult to do so. Take time to talk about the 'Forgiving Hand' art activity in your child's Religious Education journal. Ask your child to explain the 'Stop, Think, Respond' tools that they chose for this activity.

Read

Read the Parable of the Unforgiving Servant on page 86 and talk about what it teaches about forgiveness.

Invitation to Pray

Ask your child to tell you about what the statement 'forgive us our trespasses, as we forgive those who trespass against us' in the *Our Father* means. Then pray the *Our Father* together. Your child might like to show you the gestures they have learned in school for this prayer.

Be Willing

Be willing to share family stories about forgiveness. Your child may be able to include some of these stories in the Class Forgiveness Book with your permission.

Theme 10: Reconciliation | Lesson 2: God Calls Us to Forgive Others

IN SCHOOL

THIS WEEK IN SCHOOL

You are invited to think about:
- Being thankful to God for all the blessings he has given you
- The meaning of the Eucharistic Prayer
- What we give thanks for at Mass

KEY WORDS

Eucharist: The word 'Eucharist' comes from a Greek word meaning 'thanksgiving'. The Eucharist is one of the seven sacraments of the Catholic Church. The term is also often used to mean the Mass.

Eucharistic Prayer: The Eucharistic Prayer is at the heart of the Liturgy of the Eucharist, which is a key part of the Mass. It is a special prayer of thanks addressed to God the Father, which is said by the celebrant (a bishop or priest), who represents Christ, on behalf of all the people.

Consecration: Name for the part of the Mass where the bread and wine are changed into the Body and Blood of Jesus Christ.

Saviour/Redeemer: Titles for Jesus. Both words mean 'one who saves'. These titles remind us that Jesus died to save us.

THEME 11: THE MASS | LESSON 1
At Mass We Give Thanks

ABOUT BEING THANKFUL

Recall the story about the twins Jayden and Sophia and why they decided that it would be a good idea to make and send 'Thank You' cards. Why is it important to be thankful and to express our thanks? What are some of the other ways to say 'Thank you' rather than in words?

ACTIVITY

- In pairs, choose five languages and find out how to say 'Thank you' in each language. Record the words in your Religious Education journal.

SAYING THANKS AT MASS

At Mass the priest says the Eucharistic Prayer during the Liturgy of the Eucharist. This is a prayer of thanksgiving to God, which the priest, who represents Christ, says on behalf of all the people who are present. The people listen in silence as the priest thanks God, on their behalf, for all his gifts, and especially for sending Jesus to show us how to live and love as his disciples. The people pray the appropriate responses after the Consecration and at the end of the Eucharistic Prayer.

Jayden and Sophia

ABOUT EUCHARISTIC PRAYER II
There are ten Eucharistic Prayers, of which four are used most often. In this lesson we look at Eucharistic Prayer II. These are the key elements of that prayer:
- The priest addresses God and asks him to send his Spirit upon the gifts of bread and wine to make them holy.
- The priest then prays the words Jesus said at the Last Supper:

> Take this, all of you, and drink from it,
> for this is the chalice of my Blood,
> the Blood of the new and eternal covenant,
> which will be poured out for you and for many
> for the forgiveness of sins.
>
> Do this in memory of me.

- The priest recalls Jesus' death and Resurrection.
- The priest prays for the Church, which means its leaders and all its members, and for those who have died.

ACTIVITY
When the priest prays for the Church during the Eucharistic Prayer, he mentions the Pope and the bishop of the diocese.
- Name our Pope and the bishop (or archbishop) of this diocese (or archdiocese).

FOR MEMORISATION

One of the responses after the Consecration:
We proclaim your Death,
   O Lord,
and profess your Resurrection
until you come again.

Theme 11: The Mass | Lesson 1: At Mass We Give Thanks

AT HOME

DID YOU KNOW?

Jesus gave thanks to God the Father many times. For example, he thanked God for listening to his prayers when he said, 'I thank you, Father, that you listen to me' (John 11:41).

TIME TOGETHER

Chat Together
About all the things you should be thankful for in your family. Perhaps you don't thank one another often enough for all the good things that each member of the family does and the blessings each one brings to the family. Talk about and thank one another for some of those things now.

Invitation to Pray
Loving God,
You bless our family in many ways.
We thank you for the gifts of friendship and family.
Help us always to support one another.
We ask this through Christ our Lord. Amen.

Be Thankful
Be aware of all the blessings in your life and be thankful for them. Remember, too, to say 'Thanks' – to God and to others.

THIS WEEK
The children explored the importance of being thankful and the many ways we show our thankfulness to one another in daily life. They also learned about the key elements of the Eucharistic Prayer, which the priest, representing Christ, says on behalf of all the people who have come together at Mass. The Eucharistic Prayer is a prayer of thanks to God for all his gifts and for Jesus, who is our Saviour.

Read the poem 'Thanks' together.

Thanks

What can I give
To the friend who is kind,
To the one who stays with me
When I'm left behind?

And what can I give
To the teacher who'll say
'Don't worry too much.
You'll be better some day'?

And what can I give
To my loved ones who share
All the love in their hearts
In the way that they care?

'Thanks' is a word
That is really quite small.
It's the gift that I give
To show love for them all.

Grow in Love | Fourth Class/Primary 6

THEME 11: THE MASS | LESSON 2

We Go from Mass to Live Like Jesus

ABOUT GIVING AND RECEIVING

We give and receive every day. We can give someone something that helps them to feel good or something that does not help them to feel good. Can you recall something you gave to someone already today and something that you received? Do you think that what you gave helped the other person to feel better? Did what you received help you to feel good? Why or why not? What happens if a person only wants to receive all the time?

ACTIVITY
- In pairs, talk about some of the things you give and receive every day. Were you surprised by the number of things you thought of?
- Record some of the things you identified in your Religious Education journal.

IN SCHOOL

THIS WEEK IN SCHOOL

You are invited to think about:
- What you give and receive every day
- The meaning of the Dismissal Rite at Mass
- The ways in which you continue the mission of Jesus

KEY WORDS

Celebrant: The person who leads the people in celebrating the sacraments. At Mass the celebrant is usually a bishop or a priest, but certain parts of the Mass may also be conducted by a deacon.

Deacon: An ordained minister in the Church who is not a priest but who is allowed to carry out certain duties, such as assisting the bishop or priest in the celebration of the Eucharist. All those preparing for the priesthood serve as deacons before they become priests.

Rite: An important action that happens in the church and that is done in a similar way on every occasion. The different rites performed at Mass usually involve both words and actions.

Theme 11: The Mass | Lesson 2: We Go from Mass to Live Like Jesus

IN SCHOOL

FOR MEMORISATION

The Concluding Rites at Mass
Celebrant: The Lord be with you.
All: And with your spirit.

Celebrant: May Almighty God bless you, the Father, + and the Son and the Holy Spirit.
All: Amen.

Celebrant: Go forth, the Mass is ended.
All: Thanks be to God.

GIVING AND RECEIVING AT MASS

At Mass there is much giving and receiving. For example, we receive the Word of God in the readings that are read aloud during the Liturgy of the Word. At Holy Communion we receive the Body of Christ and we give thanks. We give a blessing of peace to others during the sign of peace, and before we leave the church the priest gives us a blessing.
- How can you prepare to receive the Word of God at Mass?
- How can you prepare to receive the Body of Christ at Mass?

ACTIVITY
- In your Religious Education journal record some of the giving and receiving that happens at Mass.

ABOUT THE CONCLUDING RITES AT MASS

At the end of Mass the priest (or deacon) blesses the people in the name of the Father, the Son and the Holy Spirit. As he does so he makes the Sign of the Cross over the people, and the people make the Sign of the Cross. Then, just as Jesus sent his disciples to continue his mission, the celebrant sends the people out to continue the mission of Jesus in the world today. This is known as the Dismissal Rite. The celebrant may use a number of different phrases, the most common being 'Go forth, the Mass is ended', and the people respond 'Thanks be to God'.

THIS WEEK

The children explored how, when we participate in the celebration of the Eucharist, we remember all that God has done for us and we give thanks. We remember especially that God sent his Son, Jesus, to show us how to live and how to love, and that Jesus died on the Cross for us. In Holy Communion we receive the Body of Christ and at the end of Mass we are sent out to continue the mission of Jesus in the world today.

Pray this prayer, which is called the *Sanctus*, together. It is prayed at Mass during the Eucharistic Prayer.

> **Sanctus**
> Holy, Holy, Holy Lord God of hosts.
> Heaven and earth are full of your glory.
> Hosanna in the highest.
> Blessed is he who comes in the name of the Lord.
> Hosanna in the highest.

AT HOME

DID YOU KNOW?

Many people bless themselves when they pass a church because Jesus is present in the Blessed Sacrament reserved in the tabernacle.

TIME TOGETHER

Chat Together
About times when you gather as a family to remember and to celebrate. When did this last happen in your family? Perhaps you have photographs of the occasion that you can look at together now. Recall who was there and what memories you have of it. Then look at the picture below. Chat about what you see in it and about when those items are used at Mass.

Invitation to Pray
Jesus, I thank you for coming to me in Holy Communion. You have nourished me so I can love and serve you in my daily life. Holy Spirit, give me the grace to do this. Amen.

Remember
You can pray at any time and in any place. God is always with you, wherever you are.

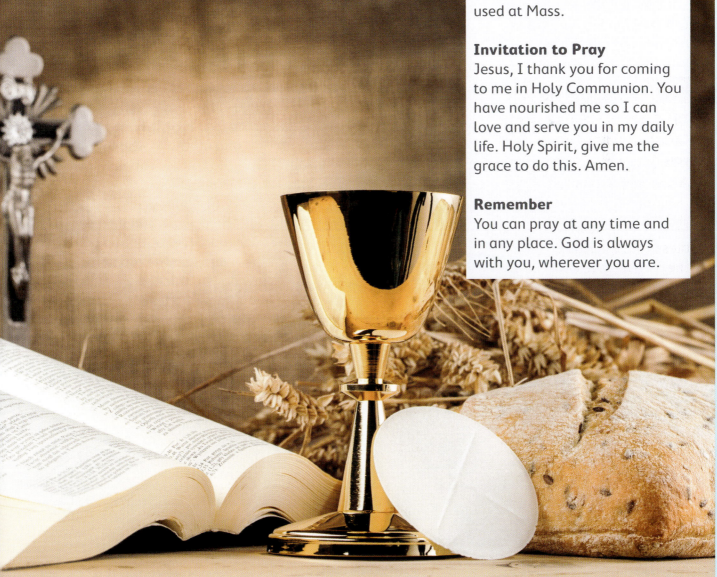

Theme 11: The Mass | Lesson 2: We Go from Mass to Live Like Jesus

IN SCHOOL

THIS WEEK IN SCHOOL

You are invited to think about:
- The cycle of life and death that applies to all living things
- St Paul's teachings about eternal life
- How you can prepare for eternal life

KEY WORDS

Eternal life: Life everlasting with God, which is promised to all those who love God and live in the way Jesus showed us.

Heaven: Term used to describe the happiness of eternal life with God.

All Saints' Day: A day (1 November) when we honour all the saints. This feast is also known as the Feast of All Saints or the Solemnity of All Saints.

All Souls' Day: A day (2 November) when we remember and pray for all those who have died. This feast is also known as the Commemoration of All the Faithful Departed.

SEASONAL LESSON 1: ETERNAL LIFE

Life with God Forever in Heaven

ABOUT BEING WITH SOMEONE IN PERSON

Recall the story about Katie and her family waiting for the return of baby Simon and his parents from Australia. They saw lots of photographs of the new baby and they were able to hear and see him on Skype, but they couldn't wait to meet him in person and really get to know him.

- Have you ever talked to anyone that you hadn't seen for a long time on Skype or Facetime or any other form of social media? Was it as good as seeing them in person? Why or why not?

ABOUT LIFE AND DEATH

The earth is full of living things, all of which are precious gifts from God. While all living things enjoy a certain span of life on earth, eventually they die and new life emerges, and the cycle of life and death continues. Think of the leaves that fall from the trees in autumn. The nutrients that the dead leaves contain nourish the new life that bursts forth in springtime.

For human beings, death is not the end either. Just as Jesus died and returned to his Father in heaven, those of us who love God and live in the way Jesus taught, with the help of God's grace, can look forward to a new and glorious life with God and all those who love him in heaven. Jesus told us that this is what God wants for each one of us.

- Recall people whom you loved who have died. Tell the child sitting next to you how you would feel about being reunited with them again in the next life.
- How do you think you would feel about meeting God?

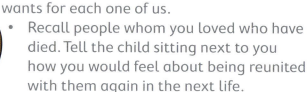

Katie sees a photograph of Simon

Grow in Love | Fourth Class/Primary 6

IN SCHOOL

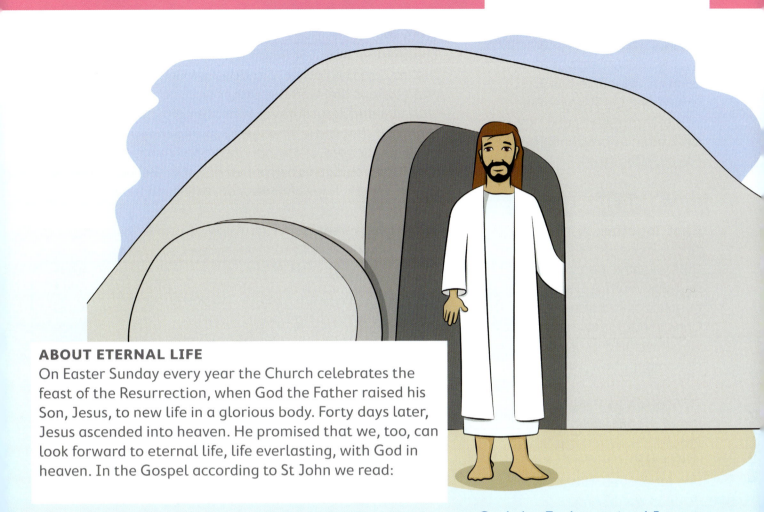

God the Father raised Jesus to new life in a glorious body

ABOUT ETERNAL LIFE
On Easter Sunday every year the Church celebrates the feast of the Resurrection, when God the Father raised his Son, Jesus, to new life in a glorious body. Forty days later, Jesus ascended into heaven. He promised that we, too, can look forward to eternal life, life everlasting, with God in heaven. In the Gospel according to St John we read:

> For God loved the world so much that he gave his only Son, so that everyone who believes in him may not die but have eternal life. For God did not send his Son into the world to be its judge, but to be its saviour. (John 3:16-17)

After the risen Jesus had gone back to heaven, St Paul wrote a letter to the people of Corinth, the Corinthians, in which he passed on to them the Good News that Jesus had taught about eternal life. He told the people that when they would finally be united with God in heaven, all their questions would be answered. He said:

> What we see now is like a dim image in a mirror; then we shall see face to face. What I know now is only partial; then it will be complete – as complete as God's knowledge of me. (1 Corinthians 13:12)

FOR MEMORISATION

Prayer for those who have died
Eternal rest grant unto them, O Lord,
and let perpetual light shine upon them. Amen.

ACTIVITY
- In your Religious Education journal draw a picture of what it might be like to be with God in heaven. Use colours, shapes, designs or words.

Seasonal Lesson 1: Eternal Life | Life with God Forever in Heaven

AT HOME

DID YOU KNOW?
Each year the Feast of All Saints is celebrated on 1 November. On 2 November we celebrate All Souls' Day, or the Commemoration of All the Faithful Departed.

TIME TOGETHER

Chat Together
About some of the saints that you have heard about. Perhaps your local school or parish is called after a saint. Chat about family members who have died and what you remember about them.

Invitation to Pray
Prayer for those who have died
Eternal rest grant unto them,
　O Lord,
and let perpetual light shine
　upon them. Amen.

Be Hopeful
Be hopeful that one day you will be united with Jesus, Mary, the saints and all those people you loved who have died when you go to your final home in heaven.

THIS WEEK
The children heard St Paul's teachings about eternal life. Just as God the Father raised Jesus from death to a new and glorious life, God the Father wants us, too, to live with him and Jesus forever in heaven after we die. Jesus promised that those who love God and their neighbour can look forward to eternal life. Pope Francis often says, 'Don't let yourselves be robbed of hope.' Because of Jesus Christ, we can hope that we, too, will go to heaven.

Read these verses from Psalm 139 together:

> **Psalm 139:1-6**
> Lord, you have examined me and you know me.
> You know everything I do;
> 　from far away you understand all my thoughts.
> You see me, whether I am working or resting;
> 　you know all my actions.
> Even before I speak,
> 　you already know what I will say.
> You are all around me on every side;
> 　you protect me with your power.
> Your knowledge of me is too deep;
> 　it is beyond my understanding.

Memorial lanterns are lit in graveyards on All Saints' Day in Poland

96　　　　Grow in Love | Fourth Class/Primary 6

IN SCHOOL

SEASONAL LESSON 2: ST BRIGID
Remembering St Brigid

ABOUT ST BRIGID

St Brigid, who is also known as 'Mary of the Gael' (Mary of the Irish), was born near Faughart in County Louth around the year 454. She spent most of her life in Kildare, where she eventually built an abbey on a hill near an oak tree. Since that time it has been a place of prayer and pilgrimage.

When she was a young girl Brigid heard St Patrick preaching about God and so she was among the first generation of Christians in Ireland. There are many stories associated with St Brigid, all of which show her to have been a person who loved God and who brought God's love to others, especially to those who were most in need. She was also a healer, a teacher and someone who cared deeply for the environment.

ABOUT THE LEGENDS ASSOCIATED WITH ST BRIGID

A legend is a story that has been passed down from generation to generation, which may or may not be true in all its details. Legends were often used in times past to help people to understand and remember things that were true, just as Jesus used parables to help people to understand his message. The events in the legends were usually very memorable, which made it easy for people to pass them on and keep the stories alive. There are many legends associated with St Brigid. All of them paint a picture of what the real St Brigid was like and of the qualities people saw in her.

THIS WEEK IN SCHOOL

You are invited to think about:
- The stories and symbols associated with St Brigid
- Praying to St Brigid
- How people keep the spirit of St Brigid alive today

KEY WORDS

Staff: In olden times a shepherd used a staff, which was a curved stick, to steer sheep that had strayed back to the flock. Today, bishops carry a staff to reflect their role as shepherds leading people to God. Paintings of St Brigid often show her holding a staff in her hand.

Abbey: Name of the place where monks and nuns usually live.

Brigid tells the chieftain about Jesus

Seasonal Lesson 2: St Brigid | Remembering St Brigid

IN SCHOOL

FOR MEMORISATION

Prayer associated with the St Brigid's Cross
May the blessing of God and the Trinity be on this cross, and on the home where it hangs and on everyone who looks at it.

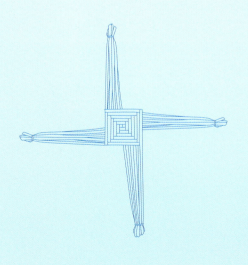

DISCUSS
- In pairs, recall the legend of St Brigid and the dying chieftain. Talk about what you learned from that story about the kind of person St Brigid was and how much her faith meant to her.
- Then recall the legend of St Brigid and the two sisters returning on horseback to the Abbey. What do you think the people who told that story wanted others to know about St Brigid?

ACTIVITY
- Find out if there are any schools and churches in your diocese or archdiocese that have St Brigid as their patron saint. Record those in your Religious Education journal.

ABOUT ST BRIGID'S CROSS
St Brigid is known for her love of people who were poor and sick and for her love of nature, animals and the land. Today, the St Brigid's Cross is still hung in homes, schools and other places as a protection against fire and theft, sickness and disease, and as a blessing on all who enter and leave these places. Sometimes farmers hang the St Brigid's Cross in stables and other places where animals are kept so that St Brigid will protect the animals.
- In pairs, chat about places where you might hang a St Brigid's Cross.
- Can you remember anywhere you have seen a St Brigid's Cross?
- Do you know anyone who is called after St Brigid?

98   Grow in Love | Fourth Class/Primary 6

THIS WEEK

The children heard stories and legends about St Brigid. They explored how the influence of this Irish saint has helped many people to grow in love of God and others since ancient times. The children saw St Brigid's crosses being woven. They were also taught that they can pray to St Brigid to ask God to help them, too, to appreciate the wonders of creation and to be active in loving their neighbours, as Brigid did. St Brigid is a role model for the life of a Christian.

Read the words of this prayer together:

> Brigid, woman of faith and courage,
> Inspire us to grow in love
> Of God and of others,
> And to share that love
> As you did.
> We ask this through Jesus Christ our Lord. Amen.

AT HOME

DID YOU KNOW?
The feast of St Brigid, Lá Fhéile Bríde, is celebrated on 1 February every year.

TIME TOGETHER

Chat Together
About St Brigid and invite your child to tell you some of the stories they have heard about her.

Invitation to Pray
May St Brigid's life be an example for us in our own lives.
May her faith inspire us now and every day.
We ask this through Christ our Lord. Amen.

Remember
Remember St Brigid especially on 1 February, St Brigid's Day, or Lá Fhéile Bríde.

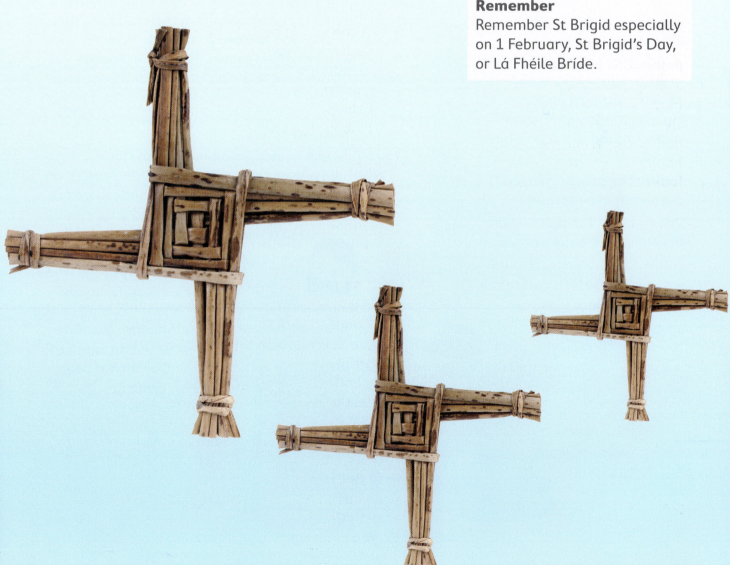

Seasonal Lesson 2: St Brigid | Remembering St Brigid

IN SCHOOL

THIS WEEK IN SCHOOL

You are invited to think about:
- How Muslims believe in one God
- How the daily prayer practices of Muslims compare with those of Christians
- How Muslims' reverence for the Qur'an challenges Christians to look at their reverence for the Bible

KEY WORDS

Islam: The name of the religion of Muslims.

Allah: Muslims believe in God, whom they call Allah. Allah is the Arabic word for God.

Qur'an: The name of the sacred text of Muslims.

Prophet Muhammad: Muslims believe that God revealed the words of the Qur'an to the prophet Muhammad through the angel Gabriel. Muhammad passed on these words, and out of this developed the faith of Islam.

Imam: The person who leads the prayer in a mosque.

Wudu area: The place where Muslims wash before prayer.

Hijab: Scarf worn by Muslim women and girls to cover their hair and neck.

SEASONAL LESSON 3: ISLAM

Our Muslim Brothers and Sisters

ABOUT ISLAM AND PLACES OF WORSHIP

Recall the stories of the three friends Muireann, Eli and Salma from the Catholic, Jewish and Muslim faith traditions. Chat about all the things you remember learning about the Muslim faith in previous *Grow in Love* programmes.

Then chat about the places of worship of these three faith traditions. These questions may help you: What is a mosque and what happens there? Who worships in a synagogue? Where is Mass usually celebrated?

ACTIVITY

Recall the story of Salma's visit to her gran in England and of how she wrote letters to her friend Muireann about her adventures there. In one of her letters Salma told Muireann about her visit to a mosque, and when Salma returned from England she invited Muireann to go with her and her parents to Friday prayers in their local mosque.

- Based on what you learned from Salma's letter and from the story of Muireann's visit to the mosque, in your Religious Education journal sketch the inside of a mosque or record your impression of what a person would find in a mosque. Label the drawing to show the various features.
- You might like to include some or all of these: the main prayer area, which has a lined carpet on which the people pray (Remember that there are no seats in this area. The women and girls usually go to a separate area to pray, but they can also pray behind the men and boys); the wudu area; the mihrab; the imam standing on the minbar; a wooden stand on which the Qur'an has been placed.

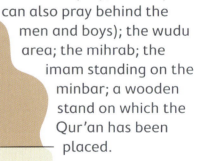

100   Grow in Love | Fourth Class/Primary 6

IN SCHOOL

ABOUT THE QUR'AN

All religions have sacred texts, which the people revere and treat with great respect. The sacred text for Jews is the Torah and for Christians it is the Bible. The Qur'an is the sacred text for Muslims. Muslims believe that the words of the Qur'an are the words of God, which were revealed to the prophet Muhammad by the angel Gabriel. All Muslim beliefs and practices are rooted in the Qur'an and the teachings of the prophet Muhammad.

The Qur'an is written in Arabic and, when it is read aloud in the mosque, Muslims listen very attentively to the words. Sometimes the Qur'an is placed on a special stand for the reading.

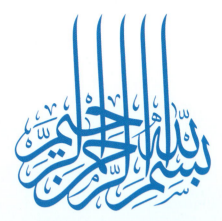

Arabic calligraphy for *Bismillah*, which means 'In the name of Allah'. Muslims say this before doing any task that they want Allah to bless

ABOUT MUSLIM PRAYER

Muslims pray to Allah five times each day:
- Before sunrise (*Fajr*)
- After noon (*Dhuhr*)
- In the afternoon (*Asr*)
- After the sun has finished setting (*Maghrib*)
- In the evening (*Isha*)

Prayers can be said individually at home or elsewhere, or with other worshippers at the mosque. In the mosque, the imam leads the prayers. Prayers are said in Arabic. Muslims always pray facing the city of Mecca in Saudi Arabia. Muslims pray with their body as well as with words and chants. *Rak'ah* is the name for the special actions or movements that Muslims perform when praying. Each of these actions has a particular meaning.

- Muslims use gestures when they pray. So do Catholics. Recall some of the gestures we use at Mass, for example, when we pray the *Our Father*, as the Gospel is being introduced, and for the sign of peace. Recall whether the people sit, stand or kneel as these prayers are said.

ACTIVITY
- In your Religious Education journal record one thing you like about the Muslim *Rak'ah* and one thing you like about one of the prayers with gestures that you learned earlier in this *Grow in Love* programme.

Seasonal Lesson 3: Islam | Our Muslim Brothers and Sisters

AT HOME

DID YOU KNOW?
Allah is the Arabic word for God. Christian Arabs also refer to God as Allah.

TIME TOGETHER

Chat Together
Ask your child to tell you what they have learned about Islam, the religion of Muslims.

Invitation to Pray
Loving God, you created all people in your image, and so all people are your children. Guide us to love and respect all people, including those who have different religious beliefs from us.

Be Thankful
Be thankful for your Muslim brothers and sisters.

THIS WEEK
The children learned more about the religion of Muslims, which is called Islam. Muslims believe in God, whom they call Allah (the Arabic name for God). They believe that God revealed the Qur'an, the sacred text of Islam, to the prophet Muhammad and that the Qur'an is the unchanged word of God. The Qur'an requires that all Muslims pray five times a day. Friday is a special day of prayer, when many Muslims pray at the mosque.

These are some Arabic prayers that Muslim children say in different situations:

> *Assalam Alaykum* ('Peace be upon you') – said as a greeting on meeting someone.
>
> *Wa alaykum salaam wa rahmatu Allahi wa Barakatuhu* ('And may peace, mercy and blessings be upon you') – said in reply to another person's greeting.
>
> *Al-hamdulilah* ('All praise is due to God') – said after eating or when a person is happy about something that has happened to them.
>
> *Yarhamuku Allah* ('May God have mercy on you') – said to a person after they have sneezed.
>
> *Subhan Allah* ('Glory be to God, the One who is perfect') – said when someone is amazed by something.

IN SCHOOL

SEASONAL LESSON 4: GROW IN LOVE

How We Have Grown in Love!

Share the thoughts that come to your mind when you look at each of the pictures on this and the next page.

THIS WEEK IN SCHOOL

You are invited to think about:
- All that you have learned this year in *Grow in Love*
- Your favourite images, stories, poems and songs
- Saying thanks to God and to all those who have helped you this year

Seasonal Lesson 4: Grow in Love | How We Have Grown in Love! 103

IN SCHOOL

THIS WEEK
The children were offered an opportunity to reflect back on the school year. They revised the themes they covered in the programme and engaged creatively with them. They celebrated all that they had learned as they experienced their own growth in God's love and their trust in him.

Read these verses from Psalm 138 together:

> **Psalm 138:1-2, 3, 8**
> I thank you, Lord, with all my heart;
> I sing praise to you before the gods…
> I … bow down, and praise your name
> because of your constant love and faithfulness.
> You answered me when I called to you;
>   with your strength you strengthened me.
>
> You will do everything you have promised;
>   Lord, your love is eternal.
> Complete the work that you have begun.

AT HOME

DID YOU KNOW?
God wants us to 'grow in love' each day.

TIME TOGETHER

Chat Together
About all that has happened this year. Tell your child some of the things you have noticed about how he or she has grown and developed. Chat about your favourite things from this year's *Grow in Love* programme.

Invitation to Pray
Loving God, Creator of all, we thank you for all that we have learned in the *Grow in Love* programme. Holy Spirit, give us the grace to help us build your kingdom here on earth by acting justly and with love. Mary our Mother, lead us to Jesus so that we may come to know and follow him. Amen.

Be Attentive
Remember that God is always with us. He created us as unique human beings. He knows each of us by name. Be alert to hear what God is saying to you now. Take time to thank God for his love.

Seasonal Lesson 4: Grow in Love | How We Have Grown in Love!

Prayers

Sign of the Cross
In the name of the Father,
and of the Son,
and of the Holy Spirit. Amen.

Comhartha na Croise
In ainm an Athar,
agus an Mhic,
agus an Spioraid Naoimh. Áiméan.

Glory be to the Father
Glory be to the Father,
and to the Son,
and to the Holy Spirit;
as it was in the beginning,
is now, and ever shall be,
world without end. Amen.

Glóir don Athair
Glóir don Athair,
agus don Mhac,
agus don Spiorad Naomh,
Mar a bhí ó thús,
mar atá anois
agus mar a bheas go brách,
le saol na saol. Áiméan.

Morning Prayer
Father in heaven, you love me,
You're with me night and day.
I want to love you always
In all I do and say.
I'll try to please you, Father.
Bless me through the day. Amen.

Night Prayer
God, our Father, I come to say
Thank you for your love today.
Thank you for my family,
And all the friends you give to me.
Guard me in the dark of night,
And in the morning send your light.
Amen.

Grace before Meals
Bless us, O God, as we sit together.
Bless the food we eat today.
Bless the hands that made the food.
Bless us, O God. Amen.

Grace after Meals
Thank you, God, for the food we have
eaten.
Thank you, God, for all our friends.
Thank you, God, for everything.
Thank you, God. Amen.

Prayer to Guardian Angel
Angel sent by God to guide me,
Be my light and walk beside me;
Be my guardian and protect me;
On the paths of life direct me. Amen.

Our Father
Our Father, who art in heaven,
hallowed be thy name;
thy kingdom come,
thy will be done
on earth as it is in heaven.
Give us this day our daily bread,
and forgive us our trespasses,
as we forgive those who trespass
against us;
and lead us not into temptation,
but deliver us from evil. Amen.

An Phaidir
Ár nAthair, ata ar neamh,
Go naofar d'ainm,
Go dtaga do ríocht,
Go ndéantar do thoil ar an talamh
Mar a dhéantar ar neamh.
Ár n-arán laethúil tabhair dúinn inniu,
Agus maith dúinn ár bhfiacha,
Mar a mhaithimidne dár bhféichiúna
féin,
Agus ná lig sinn in gcathú,
Ach saor sinn ó olc. Áiméan.

Hail Mary
Hail Mary, full of grace,
the Lord is with thee.
Blessed art thou among women,
and blessed is the fruit of thy womb,
Jesus.
Holy Mary, Mother of God,
pray for us sinners,
now and at the hour of our death.
Amen.

Prayer to the Trinity
Praise to the Father,
Praise to the Son,
Praise to the Spirit,
The Three in One.

Prayers to the Holy Spirit
Holy Spirit, I want to do what is right.
Help me.
Holy Spirit, I want to live like Jesus.
Guide me.
Holy Spirit, I want to pray like Jesus.
Teach me.

Come, Holy Spirit, fill the hearts of
your faithful.

Enkindle in us the fire of your love.
Send forth your Spirit and we shall be
created,
And you shall renew the face of the
earth.

O, God, who has taught the hearts of
the faithful
By the light of the Holy Spirit,
Grant us in the same Spirit to be truly
wise
And ever to rejoice in his consolation,
Through Christ our Lord. Amen.

The Angelus
The angel of the Lord declared unto
Mary …
And she conceived of the Holy Spirit.
Hail Mary …
Behold the handmaid of the Lord …
Be it done unto me according to thy
Word.
Hail Mary …
And the Word was made flesh …
And dwelt among us.
Hail Mary …
Pray for us, O holy Mother of God …
That we may be made worthy of the
promises of Christ.

Lord,
fill our hearts with your love,
and as you revealed to us by an angel
the coming of your Son as man,
so lead us through his suffering and
death
to the glory of his resurrection,
for he lives and reigns with you and
the Holy Spirit,
one God for ever and ever. Amen.

Care for the Earth
God, our Creator, you have given us
the earth, and the sky and the seas.
Show us how to care for the earth, not
just for today but for ages to come.
Let no plan or work of ours damage
or destroy the beauty of your creation.
Send forth your Spirit to direct us to
care for the earth and all creation.
Amen.

Prayer on Opening the Bible
Bless me, O God, so that
In opening this Bible
I may open my mind and heart
To your Word.
May it nourish me
As it nourished Jesus. Amen.

Grow in Love | Fourth Class/Primary 6

Prayer on Closing the Bible
Bless me, O God, so that
In closing this Bible
I may enclose your Word
In my heart and in my mind
As Jesus enclosed it in his. Amen.

Apostles' Creed
I believe in God,
the Father almighty,
Creator of heaven and earth,
and in Jesus Christ, his only Son, our
Lord,
who was conceived by the Holy Spirit,
born of the Virgin Mary,
suffered under Pontius Pilate,
was crucified, died, and was buried;
he descended into hell;
on the third day he rose again from
the dead;
he ascended into heaven,
and is seated at the right hand of God
the Father almighty,
from there he will come to judge the
living and the dead.

I believe in the Holy Spirit,
the holy catholic Church,
the communion of saints,
the forgiveness of sins,
the resurrection of the body,
and life everlasting. Amen.

The Magnificat
My soul proclaims the greatness of
the Lord,
my spirit rejoices in God my Saviour;
for he has looked with favour on his
lowly servant,
and from this day all generations will
call me blessed.
The Almighty has done great things
for me:
holy is his name.
He has mercy on those who fear him
in every generation.
He has shown the strength of his arm,
he has scattered the proud in their
conceit.
He has cast down the mighty from
their thrones,
and has lifted up the lowly.
He has filled the hungry with good
things,
and has sent the rich away empty.
He has come to the help of his servant
Israel
for he has remembered his promise of
mercy,
the promise he made to our fathers,
to Abraham and his children for ever.

The Memorare
Remember, O most gracious Virgin
Mary,
that never was it known that anyone
who fled to your protection,
implored your help or sought your
intercession was left unaided.
Inspired with this confidence, I fly
unto you,
O Virgin of virgins, my Mother.
To you do I come. Before you I stand,
sinful and sorrowful.
O Mother of the Word Incarnate,
despise not my petitions,
but in your mercy hear and answer
me. Amen.

Prayer for those who have died
Eternal rest grant unto them, O Lord,
and let perpetual light shine upon
them. Amen.

Prayer of Commendation
To you, O Lord, we commend the soul
of (name) your servant;
in the sight of this world he/she is
now dead;
in your sight may he/she live for ever.
Forgive whatever sins he/she
committed through human
weakness
and in your goodness grant him/her
everlasting peace.
We ask this through Christ our Lord.
Amen.

St Patrick's Breastplate
Christ be with me,
Christ be beside me,
Christ be before me,
Christ be behind me,
Christ be at my right hand,
Christ be at my left hand,
Christ be with me wherever I go,
Christ be my friend, for ever and ever.
Amen.

Act of Sorrow
O my God, I thank you for loving me.
I am sorry for all my sins; for not
loving others and not loving you.
Help me to live like Jesus and not sin
again. Amen.

Prayer for Forgiveness
O my God, help me to remember the
times when I didn't live as Jesus
asked me to.
Help me to be sorry and to try again.
Amen.

Prayer after Forgiveness
O my God, thank you for forgiving me.
Help me to love others.
Help me to live as Jesus asked me to.
Amen.

Prayer before Holy Communion
Lord Jesus, come to me.
Lord Jesus, give me your love.
Lord Jesus, come to me and give me
yourself.

Lord Jesus, friend of children, come
to me.
Lord Jesus, you are my Lord and my
God.
Praise to you, Lord Jesus Christ.
Amen.

Prayer after Holy Communion
Lord Jesus, I love and adore you.
You're a special friend to me.
Welcome, Lord Jesus, O welcome,
Thank you for coming to me.

Thank you, Lord Jesus, O thank you
For giving yourself to me.
Make me strong to show your love
Wherever I may be.

Be near me, Lord Jesus, I ask you to
stay
Close by me forever and love me, I
pray.
Bless all of us children in your loving
care
And bring us to heaven to live with
you there.

I'm ready now, Lord Jesus,
to show how much I care.
I'm ready now to give your love
At home and everywhere. Amen.

Journey Prayer
Arise with me in the morning,
Travel with me through each day,
Welcome me on my arrival.
God, be with me all the way. Amen.

Mission Prayer
May all the children
In the world
Share love
Share friendship and live
In the peace
Of God's love
Now and forever.

Grow in Love | Prayers

Ár bPaidir Misiúnta
Go roinne
Gach páiste ar domhan
Grá agus cairdeas,
Agus go maire siad
I síocháin ghrá Dé
Anois agus choíche.

Prayers for the Mass

INTRODUCTORY RITES
Celebrant: In the name of the Father, and of the Son, and of the Holy Spirit.
People: Amen.

Greetings
Celebrant: The grace of our Lord Jesus Christ,
and the love of God,
and the communion of the Holy Spirit
be with you all.
Or
Grace to you and peace from God our Father
and the Lord Jesus Christ.
Or
The Lord be with you.
People: And with your spirit.

Penitential Act A
I confess to almighty God
and to you, my brothers and sisters,
that I have greatly sinned,
in my thoughts and in my words,
in what I have done and in what I have failed to do,
(*striking breast, say*)
through my fault, through my fault,
through my most grievous fault;
(*then continue*)
therefore I ask blessed Mary ever-Virgin,
all the Angels and Saints,
and you, my brothers and sisters,
to pray for me to the Lord our God.

Penitential Act B
Celebrant: Have mercy on us, O Lord.
People: For we have sinned against you.
Celebrant: Show us, O Lord, your mercy.
People: And grant us your salvation.

Lord, Have Mercy
Celebrant: Lord, have mercy.
People: Lord, have mercy.
Celebrant: Christ, have mercy.
People: Christ, have mercy.
Celebrant: Lord, have mercy.

People: Lord, have mercy.
Kyrie Eleison
Celebrant: Kyrie, eleison.
All: Kyrie, eleison.
Celebrant: Christe, eleison.
All: Christe, eleison.

Gloria
Glory to God in the highest,
and on earth peace to people of good will.

We praise you,
we bless you,
we adore you,
we glorify you,
we give you thanks for your great glory,
Lord God, heavenly King,
O God, almighty Father.

Lord Jesus Christ, Only Begotten Son,
Lord God, Lamb of God, Son of the Father,
you take away the sins of the world,
    have mercy on us;
you take away the sins of the world,
    receive our prayer;
you are seated at the right hand of the Father,
    have mercy on us.

For you alone are the Holy One,
you alone are the Lord,
you alone are the Most High,
Jesus Christ,
with the Holy Spirit,
in the glory of God the Father.
Amen.

LITURGY OF THE WORD
After the Readings
Reader: The word of the Lord.
People: Thanks be to God.

Before the Gospel
Reader: The Lord be with you.
People: And with your spirit.
Reader: A reading from the holy Gospel according to (*name*).
People: Glory to you, O Lord.

After the Gospel
Celebrant: The Gospel of the Lord.
People: Praise to you, Lord Jesus Christ.
People: Praise and honour to you Lord Jesus. (*Lenten Season*)

Prayer of the Faithful
Reader: Lord, hear us.
All: Lord, graciously hear us.
Or
Reader: We pray to the Lord.
Response: Lord, hear our prayer.

LITURGY OF THE EUCHARIST
Celebrant: Blessed are you, Lord God of all creation,
for through your goodness we have received
the bread we offer you:
fruit of the earth and work of human hands,
it will become for us the bread of life.
People: Blessed be God for ever.

Celebrant: Blessed are you, Lord God of all creation,
for through your goodness we have received
the wine we offer you:
fruit of the vine and work of human hands,
it will become our spiritual drink.
People: Blessed be God for ever.

Celebrant: Pray, brethren (brothers and sisters),
that my sacrifice and yours
may be acceptable to God,
the almighty Father.
People: May the Lord accept the sacrifice at your hands
for the praise and glory of his name,
for our good
and the good of all his holy Church.

Preface Dialogue
Celebrant: The Lord be with you.
People: And with your spirit.

Celebrant: Lift up your hearts.
People: We lift them up to the Lord.

Celebrant: Let us give thanks to the Lord our God.
People: It is right and just.

Sanctus
Holy, Holy, Holy Lord God of hosts.
Heaven and earth are full of your glory.
Hosanna in the highest.
Blessed is he who comes in the name of the Lord.
Hosanna in the highest

Mystery of Faith (Memorial Acclamation)
Celebrant: The mystery of faith.
People: We proclaim your Death, O Lord,
and profess your Resurrection
until you come again.
Or
When we eat this Bread and drink this Cup,
we proclaim your Death, O Lord,
until you come again.
Or
Save us, Saviour of the world,
for by your Cross and Resurrection
you have set us free.
Or
My Lord and my God.

COMMUNION RITE
The Lord's Prayer
Celebrant: At the Saviour's command
and formed by divine teaching,
we dare to say:
People: Our Father, who art in heaven,
hallowed be thy name;
thy kingdom come,
thy will be done
on earth as it is in heaven.
Give us this day our daily bread,
and forgive us our trespasses,
as we forgive those who trespass against us;
and lead us not into temptation,
but deliver us from evil.
Celebrant: Deliver us, Lord, we pray,
from every evil,
graciously grant peace in our days,
that, by the help of your mercy,
we may be always free from sin
and safe from all distress,
as we await the blessed hope
and the coming of our Saviour, Jesus Christ.
People: For the kingdom,
the power and the glory are yours
now and for ever.

Sign of Peace
Celebrant: The peace of the Lord be with you always.
People: And with your spirit.
Celebrant: Let us offer each other the sign of peace.

Agnus Dei
Lamb of God, you take away the sins of the world,
have mercy on us.
Lamb of God, you take away the sins of the world,
have mercy on us.
Lamb of God, you take away the sins of the world,
grant us peace.

Invitation to Holy Communion
Celebrant: Behold the Lamb of God,
behold him who takes away the sins of the world.
Blessed are those called to the supper of the Lamb.
People: Lord, I am not worthy
that you should enter under my roof,
but only say the word
and my soul shall be healed.

When Receiving Communion
Celebrant: The Body of Christ.
People: Amen.

CONCLUDING RITES
Celebrant: The Lord be with you.
People: And with your spirit.
Celebrant: May almighty God bless you,
the Father, and the Son, and the Holy Spirit.
People: Amen.

Dismissal
Celebrant: Go forth, the Mass is ended.
Or
Go and announce the Gospel of the Lord.
Or
Go in peace, glorifying the Lord by your life.
Or
Go in peace.
People: Thanks be to God.

Grow in Love | Prayers

Acknowledgements

All Scripture quotations taken from *The Catholic Children's Bible*, Saint Mary's Press, Minnesota, adapted from the Good News Translation © 1992 American Bible Society. All rights reserved.

Excerpts from the English translation of *The Roman Missal* © 2010, International Commission on English in the Liturgy Corporation (ICEL); excerpt from the English translation of the Prayer of Commendation from Order of Christian Funerals © 1985, ICEL. All rights reserved. Used with permission.

'The New School Year' (p. 6) by Finbar O'Connor, copyright © Veritas Publications.

'Imagine' (p. 15, one verse), 'The Mustard Seed' (p. 21), 'Choice' (p. 51), 'Remember' (p. 57), 'Making Peace' (p. 75), and 'Thanks' (p. 90) by Christy Kenneally, copyright © Christy Kenneally. Used with permission.

'Love of God and Neighbour' (p. 24), 'Stabat Mater' (p. 60), 'The Risen Jesus' (p. 63), 'Pentecost: I Was There' (p. 66), and 'Us' (p. 69) by Dr Clare Maloney. Used with permission.

'Christmas Eve' (p. 33) from *Feelings and Things* by Edna Kingsley Wallace.

Information in the 'Did You Know?' on page 39 sourced from *http://life-in-saudiarabia.blogspot.ie*.

'Trees' (p. 45) by Joyce Kilmer (1886-1918).

'Lovely Things' (p. 54) by H. M. Sarson, sourced from *The Book of 1000 Poems: The Classic Collection for Children*, Collins Educational, London.

Extract from journal of Maura Lee (p. 72) used with permission.

Information in the 'Did You Know?' on page 81 sourced from *Sacred Song in America: Religion, Music, and Public Culture* by Stephen A Marini, University of Illinois Press, Urbana and Chicago, copyright 2003 by the Board of the Trustees of the University of Illinois.

Picture Credits:
p. 5: © Estate of Evie Hone / IVARO, Dublin (2017). Photo: Bro. Jeffrey Pioquinto, SJ.
p. 10: Pope Francis © andykatz/Thinkstock; Pope John XXIII © Universal Images Group North America LLC / DeAgostini / Alamy Stock Photo; Pope John Paul II © RealyEasyStar/ Fotografia Felici / Alamy Stock Photo
p. 12: Photo: David Monniaux
p. 14 & 15: © 2009 The Board of Trinity College Dublin
p. 28: © Look and Learn
p. 33: Photo: Ann Bracken
p. 34: Photo: © Agustín Garza
p. 57: Photo: sedmak
p. 59: Courtesy of St Mel's Cathedral, artist Ken Thompson and photographer Donal Murphy
p. 63: Photo: Paul Clayton-Lea
p. 68: Photo: ITAR-TASS Photo Agency / Alamy Stock Photo
p. 73: Athlone Methodist Church (photo: Dantadd); St Vincent's Catholic Church (photo: Jim Linwood); St Philip & St James Anglican Church (photo: DubhEire); Greek Orthodox Church of the Annunciation (photo: Lisa Cassidy); Abbey Presbyterian Church (photo: Kaihsu Tai)
p. 76: Photo: Stephen Barnes / Alamy Stock Photo
p. 77: Photo: Godong / Alamy Stock Photo
p. 80: Photo: Nheyob
p. 84: RealyEasyStar/ Fotografia Felici / Alamy Stock Photo

Every effort has been made to contact the copyright holders of the material reproduced in *Grow in Love*. If any infringement has occurred, the owners of such copyright are requested to contact the publishers.